Philosophy of Friendship

Philosophy of Friendship © Copyright 2020 by Dr. Shirley Hughes

Cover design © David L. Hughes

All rights reserved. No part of this work may be reproduced or stored in an information retrieval system (other than for purposes of review) without prior written permission by the copyright holder.

A catalogue record of this book is available from the British Library

First Edition: June 2020

ISBN: 978-1-84375-626-2

This is a work of fiction. Names, characters, places and incidents are the product of the author's imagination or are used fictitiously, and any resemblance to any actual persons, living or dead, events, or locales is entirely coincidental.

To order additional copies of this book please visit:
http://www.prestige-press.com/shirleyhughes

Published by: Prestige Press
Email: info@prestige-press.com
Web: http://www.prestige-press.com

Other Books by the author:

Persona
In Depth Of Soul
The Choices of Being
The Grass Isn't Always Greener
Rose Tinted Glasses
Leah's Journey
The Pink Flamingo Fellowship
Bilé
Academia
Pathway To The Unconscious
Sartre – In Focus
Mooloo
The Symbolic Mask
Ghostopia
Recognising The Soul
Transformation

Philosophy of Friendship

by

Dr. Shirley Hughes

Prestige Press

Contents

1 Introduction 9
2 Contemporary Friendship 11
3 Categories Of Friendship 13
4 Eudaimonia 21
5 Philia 22
6 The Quest For Friendship 23
7 If You Want A Friend 24
8 Is Friendship Limited To Number? 25
9 Happiness And Friendship 27
10 What Are Friends For? 28
11 The Magic Of Friendship 29
12 Amy's Story 31
13 Theo And Janet's Story 48
14 Four Dimensions Of Friendship 51
15 Friendship For Education 55
16 Bringing Friendship Into Education 57
17 Closing Thoughts Re Education 61
18 Friendship With God 63
19 Thinking Ahead... The Afterlife 64
20 The Key Effects Of Friendship 65
21 Confucius On Friendship 66
22 The Friendship Between Philosophy And Science 69
23 A Co-Dependent Friendship 72
24 Friendship With Self 74
25 Cultivating Friendship 76
26 Friendship Cards 81
27 The Idea Of Friendship 82
28 Sharing The Spotlight 84
29 Philosophy Is The Friend Of Wisdom 86
30 We Don't Exist 93
31 Peace And Friendship 94
32 Moral Evolution 97
33 Party Gatherings/Events 99
34 Feminist Friendship 102
35 Friendship Examined 104
36 In Conclusion 108

Chapter 1

Introduction

It is no exaggerated statement to say that having friends especially good friends is a sure sign of success. Having friends is one of the most fundamental aspects of finding and achieving happiness. So it is safe to say we are all better off if we have a number of close friends and if we can find activities that bring us happiness that we can share with others. It is a safe bet that friendship will always be a key component of humanity. As such friends are bonded by expressions of harmony, accord, understanding and support. There are many characteristics to friendship. Friendship is a fascinating topic. On the other hand many of us have a working knowledge of its meaning and already value friendships but there is always so much more we can learn about it. Generally a friend is someone whom you like and trust and who supports you in a time of need, a person who cheers you on as you attempt some goal and yet still someone who may shout you down to bring you back to reality when you get a little too full of yourself.

We form friendships for a whole variety of reasons including the historic purposes of safety and basic survival. Friendships also serve other important purposes such as providing social inclusions and a sense of identity. People choose between alternative possible friendships by ranking the expected experiences of each potential association, then selecting the best. In particular it is believed that the main force that draws people together is social attraction defined in terms of the potential rewards whether internal or external to be gained by participating in the exchange among potential friends. Friendships are rarely one sided as it takes at least two willing individuals to negotiate the boundaries to really participate in such a friendship. There are those who provide assistance and support to one another and those who are on good terms with one another because they share certain attributes and also those who share a common interest and who participate in certain social activities. When friends have a positive experience they are more likely to maintain the friendship but when the association no longer brings happiness to all the friends it is likely to end. Friendships however forged are it seems a necessity good or bad.

Chapter 2

Contemporary Friendships

What is friendship? It links people who share dispositions and a sense of intimacy or feelings of affection and have an attachment or association with one another. As such friends are bonded by expressions of harmony, accord understanding and rapport. There are many characteristics of a friend but generally a friend is someone you like and trust and who supports you in time of need. Friends come in a variety of types and categories but they are generally described as those with whom we are attached by feelings of affection and personal regard, those who provide assistance and support, those on good terms with one another and those who may share certain core attributes with one another such as religious and cultural affiliations, or a common interest such as travel, music, a favourite sports team or an appreciation for fine dining or the fine arts.

A good starting point for discussions on friendships are the three primary types of friendships, friends of utility, friends of pleasure and friends of the good. Some friendships are likely to stay in one category indefinitely if this fits the needs of the friends involved for example many of us have work friends, friends of utility and we are quite content to keep it that way as we have no desire to spend time with them outside work. Other friendships are forged because we enjoy each other's company referred to as a friend of pleasure. Some grow from the very close, from the casual and what is called friends of the good., The meaning of friendship can vary a great deal depending on the type of friendship. The nature of a contemporary nature seems more complex than the trifold categorisation employed and can be sorted into many sub categories including those designed for normal companionship and others involving unconditional love and commitment. This integration bonds such as expectations of rewards social approval, share opinions and outlooks on life and the pleasure of social interaction provides a pivotal role in forming friendships. The type of friendship one has with others depends on the people involved, their expectation level, their needs and how much time and effort they are willing to spend on nurturing and devoting these to the friendship.

Chapter 3

Categories Of Friendship

The nature of friendship seems more complex and can be sorted into many categories including people who are attached to one another by feelings of affection or personal regard.

Casual Friends
All face to face friendships share the assumption that you have actually spent some time together and bonded to some degree, that you have shared something with one another. A casual friend would be someone with whom you spend time with where your encounters with one another are friendly but not very intimate. Casual friends will come and go while close friends may remain as acquaintances for years perhaps even a lifetime. Casual friendships may slowly fade away or may end spectacularly. Research shows that the quickest way to end a friendship is betrayal. Here the trust necessary for a continuing friendship is shattered.

Close Friends
A step above the casual friend is the close friend. Close friends may also be known as good friends. A close friend is someone you would consider part of your inner circle. This category falls in between casual friends and close friends but are not yet best friends. They can be described as those who know most about your life and have likely been through a few ups and downs with you. You may have several friends and one or two people you would consider good friends. Good friends are generally those you see and talk to the most often. We are more intimate with close friends than casual friends and we are likely to have shared some ups and

downs with close friends. However we disagree that we are likely to have just one or two people we would consider close friends. Such a quantitative limitation is reserved for the best friend category.

Best Friends
Casual friends and close friends are important but only the select few can claim the title and sentiment required and experienced by the term best friend. The best friend is the gold standard of friendship. Best friends possess all the qualities of close friends and much more. They are the friends with whom we are very close. They are our confidants and the people we can count on at all times including the good and the bad, sad and happy, excited and bored or when we just want to be with someone who will understand us. Best friends are those we value above all our other friends. Your best friend is the person you first think of when you want to share good news or when you need comforting during bad times. The apex of the hierarchy possesses a multitude of virtues including being reliable, sympathetic, trustworthy, easy going, respectful, dependable, generous, understanding, fun to be with, passionate, caring, considerate, loving, accepting and honest. Thus integrative bonds such as expectations of rewards, social approval, share opinions and outlooks on life, love and the pleasure of social attraction, provide a pivotal role in forming friendships. There are also friendships involving people who started out as good or close friends but over time begin to drift apart. In other words friendships are fluid and subject to change for any number of reasons. The type of friendship one has with others depends on the people involved, their expectations level, their needs and how much time and effort they are willing to spend on nurturing and devoting to the friendship.

Electronic - Cyber Friendships
Traditionally friendships have relied on face to face encounters with others. However with the rise of the internet friendship has expanded to the electronic and even virtual worlds. In these worlds it is possible to forge and maintain friendships without ever having met your friend face to face. Still if they are real friends,

not just Facebook friends, these friendships are based on the same characteristics of friendships found throughout history, trust, loyalty, dependability and much more. People now are relying more and more on technology to meet their needs for interaction and to seek friendships via the internet and on I-phone, phones etc. We can only venture to guess about the nature of friendships in the future. Face to face friendships will always exist at least for as long as we possess physical bodies but if technology continues to advance we may all eventually reside in a matrix type world where we and all our connections will be electronically mediated.

Until fairly recently our friendships were primarily restricted to those in close proximity to us since a minimal requirement of friendship is social interacting and interaction. However people are now able to continue old friendships or establish new friendships with little or no face to face interaction via the electronic world of inter computer communication. There is some debate whether or not a strictly electronic friendship can qualify as a real friendship. We believe that while face to face friendships are almost preferable to strictly electronic ones there is validity in electronic friendships. After all electronic friendships involve real people who choose to share feelings of affection or personal regard who support one another emotionally who share similar interests and so on. Electronic friendships then are as real as the friends make them. The key to electronic friendships like face to face friendships are voluntary participation, mutuality, sharing personal details about one another and displaying some degree of affection.

Friends with Benefits
When we were children friends with benefits might have meant someone with a swimming pool or big garden but nowadays friends with benefits means sex buddies – people who have a sexual benefit friendship without being involved with other aspects typical of an intimate friendship such as monogamy or explaining their whereabouts or daily activities to one another. Having friends with benefits may at first seem a great way to achieve happiness but of course as most people understand whenever sex is involved in a friendship things tend to become complicated.

Friends Of Friends Or Second Hand Friends

These are an interesting category of friends in that you may find them to be just as cool asyour original friend or you may find that you cannot tolerate them and despise spending time with them. When a friend introduces you to one of their other friends they may do so because they think everyone will get along or to increase the amount of time spent with both albeit at the cost of one to one time. The friend who introduces you to someone annoying however may be employing a clever strategy to ditch you both. You may find that you have more in common with a friend of a friend than with the original friend. When one gets to spend time with the second hand friend without the original they are likely to discuss the mutual friend as a means of easing the unfamiliar friendship, but eventually it may morph into a true friendship maintained even when you both move on from the original friend. If this happens the original friend becomes an ex friend.

Ex Friends

Unsurprisingly an ex friend is someone you were once friends with but are no longer. This is often due to some kind of argument and/or a betrayal. The reasons for friends breaking up dictates the level of disdain ex friends have for one another. A best friend who metaphorically stabs his friend in the back by stealing away his girlfriend via lies and other manipulations is an example of the lowest of the low ex friends. By contrast friends who simply drift apart from one another because each has developed interests that are no longer mutual are likely to hold no grudges against one another. That would be considered to be natural process. If ex close friends who parted in less than pleasant circumstances cross paths with one another a great deal of emotion is likely to be let loose. After all we expect far more from our close and best friends than we do from others. It is best to try and avidly avoid talking to an acrimoniously ex friend or at the very least try to be a better person. Civil ex friends will avoid slandering one another and keep long held secrets and just move on. Being civil might be difficult especially if you want to rip her/his head off but in the long run it's the best course of action.

Bromance Friends

The term bromance is a blend of bro - a slang term for male close or best friend and romance. The part bro reveals that this type of friendship is specifically between males. For one dictionary the term bromance is described as a close non sexual friendship between men while another describes it as a complicated love and affection shared by two straight men, a non sexual friendship between two men that are unusually close that involves the act of wooing for the purpose of becoming closer going to unusual lengths in an attempt to become close with another male friend and a close friendship between two bros to such a point where they start to seem like a couple. A bromance then is a highly formed friendship between males. While such friendships have likely occurred throughout history the word in recent times has become in vogue partly because historically it had generally been less socially acceptable for males to show emotional closeness than it has for females. Whether it would be considered as friends of the good to constitute a bromance remains an open question.

Work Friends

Many people spend more awake time with work friends than they do with most close or best friends or spouses. So it is important to have work friends if for no other reason than it makes the environment more pleasant and less stressful. Employers tend to like work friendships too as it creates a sense of camaraderie and comfort. Work friendships develop like any other friendships naturally and organically. It is natural to share some of the same interests and dispositions with some of our co-workers. There are also co-workers who we would never have been friends with if we had met under different circumstances.

Among the advantages of work friends is that they understand our job better than almost anyone else could. They have seen us at our worst for example getting yelled at by our boss or our pain from personal loss such as a breakup of a marriage or loss of a family member. They celebrate our work achievements with us and often our personal milestones such as birthdays and they encourage us to perform via such methods as brainstorming. Conversely there are some potential pitfalls with work friendships including the potential for breakup and corresponding ex friend status which might lead to a degree of discomfort with someone you have been around. Goofing around with your work friends may lead to unprofessional behaviour.

Having gained personal information about you, the work friend might use your vulnerabilities against you. If work friends start to hang out together outside of work it may throw out the work–personal life balance with other friends and loved ones and if your work friend is not in your supervisor's favour you may be guilty by association. It is now confirmed observation that people that operate in close proximity to one another as in the workplace are more likely to find themselves unknowingly attracted to one another and to go on to develop friendships. In other words the longer you are exposed to a certain person the more likely you are to be attracted to each other. It is a rather prosaic explanation of love that runs counter to the usual romantic notions which credit the emotion to providence, prayer or serendipity. Some day your prince may well come but he will be likely to be transient. Better the person opposite you in the work place. Success in friendships therefore is about having viable friendships and working at them so they are sustainable.

Situational Friends
What connects people to situational friends is a specific and likely dramatic situation. This type of friendship arises based on shared circumstances with a person with whom you probably do not have any mutual acquaintances and likely share few if any interests but you share an experience. Sharing an intense situation will often establish strong emotional ties between people. The situation in question can be pleasant such as attending a lecture, a concert or a ball game. Conversely the situation may be unpleasant such as being in the same location during a terror attack and through this a friendship was quickly cemented.

Neighbour Friendships
This category of friends is also the result of circumstances but is

generally far less intense than a situational friendship. We rarely choose our neighbours but while many people ignore their neighbours some build a friendship. Often such neighbours serve a utility purpose for instance they keep an eye on your home while you are away or they will sign for a package that is delivered while you are out but other times they bring us pleasure and may become good friends. The scenario of neighbours as close friends is used in many television soaps. A neighbour friend is someone you can call on at any time for help or assistance.

Frenemies

A frenemy is a blending of the words friend and enemy and has a dual meaning as either an enemy who pretends to be your friend or as someone who is a real friend and yet is also a rival such as team mates on a sports team who are friends but competing for the same starting position. Or perhaps a frenemy is a person with whom we outwardly show characteristics of friendship because of certain things that come with the façade but in reality we harbour feelings of resentment or rivalry and perhaps we don't even like them.

The dictionary defines a frenemy as a person who is ostensibly friendly or collegial with someone but who is actually antagonistic or competitive with them, a supposed friend who behaves in a treacherous manner and as a person who is considered as both a friend and rival. It also provides a variety of interpretations including fake friends you have for selfish reasons and purposes. This reminds us while we may see others as potential frenemies, we too can be the frenemy in order to gain something – a type of fake friend, friend of utility, people you know and are cordial with but who you don't really like and who don't really like you either, and friends you make that were once enemies because you are planning to stab them in the back. While people have dealt with frenemies throughout history, like bromance the term itself has only been introduced in the past decade or so.

Familiar Strangers

Once you have spoken to a familiar stranger – someone you see in passing but have never spoken to – you have formed a connection.

They are no longer a stranger to you. You have each acknowledged each other's existence and the next time you see them you can't just totally ignore them as you have in the past. You have to continue to make conversation even if it is just a banal nice weather we're having comment. The tendency not to interact with familiar strangers was a form of adaptation to the stimulus overload one experienced in the urban environment. These individuals are depersonalised and treated as part of the scenery rather than as people with whom to engage.

Most of us even while being friendly are still shielding much about ourselves from others even such basic information as our names, our family relations, where even we work and our education. By sharing such information with others we open up the possibility of their doing the same, at which point a friendship begins. This is also why it is easier to share such information as well as more personal information such as political beliefs, our financial situations and our sexual adventures, with strangers we are likely to meet only once, say on a plane, boat or train. Since we are not likely to meet them again we are more likely to open up, knowing that no friendship is going to form from the disclosures. However, it pays to be cautious. How can you be sure that the stranger you are talking to isn't somehow connected by just a degree or two of separation from others you have a friendship with?

Chapter 4

Eudaimonia

The question remains. Just why do we need friends and if we do need them how do such friendships arise? For without friends no one would choose to live even though he had all other goods but just why is this so? Because friends are central to overall conception of what constitutes a good life we ask the fundamental questions, what does it mean to be a human being? What goals will bring out our best? The nature of Eudaimonia, translated as happiness, but means literally having a good soul. Friendship is part of what makes for Eudaimonia and connects to the nature of what it means to be human. The good life consists of developing one's natural abilities through the use of reason and a virtuous life is where habits are formed that allow one to reach one's full potential.

Some goals such as the desire for good health, wealth or public recognition can propel us to action but such aims are not what is considered our ultimate goals. Rather they are all means to an end. The ultimate goal in life is Eudaimonia which is based on self fulfilment and self sufficiency. However we define something as self sufficient not by reference to the self alone. We do not mean a life in isolation, but who lives with parents, children, wife and friends and fellow citizens generally since we are by nature social and political beings.

Chapter 5

Philia

We are social and political beings and we cannot exist independently from everyone else. Our very development as humans is contingent on the proper or natural support given to us by other people. This leads us directly to the category of social relations and this is called philia which is the friendship of the good. The best way of defining philia is what we might call close friends, is those who hold what they have in common. Essentially philia is a personal bond you have with another being which is freely chosen because of the virtues you see in your friend.

If the only people we know are our family members our roles in life would be quite limited as would our opportunities for development. The assertion that we are by nature social and political beings is the Ancient Greek term for city but it means a body of citizens literally and it relates to the fact that almost all of us live just not in a family structure but rather within a larger political system, yet most of the people in such a system are strangers to each other. If they were related it would be clearer what roles each person is to play. Also if in fact all people in a given society were friends there would be no need for laws since we would naturally work out our differences. When people are friends they have no need of justice but when they are just they need friendship in addition. It is not possible to live only among friends for the basic reason that friendship requires commitment of time and a trusting friendship and there are natural limits to how many such connections we can make.

Chapter 6

The Quest For Friendship

Clearly in the modern era harmony forms friendship. The voluntary nature of friendship makes such relationships subject to life's whims in a manner that familial relationships are not. From childhood to high school to college or university or the military, to starting a family and starting a career to retirement and other major life events in between, we are constantly going through changes and it stands to reason that friendships will have to adjust to these life changes as well. When priorities and responsibilities change so too do most friendships. So cherishing treasured forms of friendships, close and best friends and moving on from the toxic ones, ex friends and frenemies. Life is a journey made more pleasurable by good quality friendships.

Chapter 7

If You Want A Friend

Friendships, especially friendships of the good, don't come easily and must be cultivated. In such relationships we reveal our innermost thoughts and aspirations to another. The trust between such friends is unlimited and should not be given lightly. You have to get to know the other person and that cannot be rushed. Your judgement should be a rational one not one made in haste due to expediency or pleasure. One cannot extend friendship to another person until each person has impressed the other that he is worthy of affection. Those who are quick to show the signs of friendship to one another are not true friends unless they are worthy of affection and know it is to be true. The wish to be friends can come about quickly but friendship cannot. It takes time and effort.

Chapter 8

Is Friendship Limited To Number?

Another important point is in regards to the view that we do not open up to all people because there are natural limits to the time and effort we can put into cultivating friendships. To be friends with many people in the sense of perfect friendship is impossible just as it is impossible to be in love with many people at the same time. It feels that there is definitely a natural limit to how many friends of the good one can have.

If you have a handful of such friendships in your entire life consider yourself fortunate but what might the maximum number be? Perhaps it is the largest number with whom one might be able to live together for as we noticed living together is the surest indication of friendship and it is quite obvious that it is impossible to live together with many people and divide oneself up among them. Furthermore one's friends should also be the friends of one another if they are all going to spend their days in each other's company but it is an arduous task to have this be the case among a large number of people.

Some modern thinkers are giving independent verification to these claims. Research shows that the number is necessarily finite. There is a limited amount of time and emotional capital we can distribute so we only have five slots for the most intense type of friendship. People may always say they have more than five but you can be pretty sure they are not high quality friendships. Five friends of the good is probably about all you can really sustain. To call friends of the good perfect is not to imply that there are no dangers involved in forming such friendships or no possibilities that they might end. While they are the strongest type they are not invulnerable. For instance there is always the danger that one may love a friend or that the friend moves away.

Chapter 9

Happiness And Friendship

In order to be happy we need two things, good fortune and skill. We need to develop our talents into skills so that when good fortune arrives we will know how to make the most of it. But in order to develop our skills we need the support of others most particularly of good friends. They would encourage us to make good use of our reasoning skills and to avoid vices, deficiencies and excess of behaviour that could lead us astray. The key to a good life is to achieve a happy medium between extremes and although there is no guarantee that good fortune will smile upon us nature generally allows the possibility for human beings to develop their talents in ways that will allow them to be happy and so we get by with a little help from our friends. A happy life is one where habits are formed that allow one to reach one's full potential.

Chapter 10

What Are Friends For?

There is friendship that comes about when each person is seeking fun. Their chief interest is in their own pleasure and the opportunity of the moment which the other person provides. Then there are friendships that are really strategic acquaintances where people take pleasure in each other's company only insofar as they have hopes of taking advantage of it. Then there is the true friend, not someone who is just like you but someone who isn't you and about who you care as much as you care about yourself. The sorrows of a true friend are your sorrows as their joys are yours. It makes you more vulnerable should anything befall this person but it is hugely strengthening too. You are relieved from the too small orbit of your own thoughts and worries. You expand into the life of another and together you become larger, cleverer, more resilient and more fair minded. You share virtue and cancel out each other's defects. Friendship teaches us what we ought to be. It is quite literally the best part of life.

Chapter 11

The Magic Of Friendship

The subject of friendship is the inspiration of poets, painters and writers. It is usually somewhere at the heart of the dramas we watch, the songs we listen to, the books we read. Questions regarding the success and failure of friendships fuel the conversations we have. Perhaps too consideration of friendships is involved in the choice of perfumes we wear, the clothes we buy. But even the wisest minds are at a loss to understand why and how friendship occurs between any two people. We have no more idea why one seemingly goes away while another, perhaps the meeting of an apparently odd couple, survives every test of affection. Is it then chance which determines many meetings? In part surely. Apart from the likelihood of meeting in a work place or via a friend's friend, how many chance encounters have brought people together in unlikely places, or opposite sides of the globe, in queues or gatherings where one would not usually be? Also are friendship workings a mystery? Again at least in part, for although philosophers will take pains to rationalise how friendships flourish or why they take root at all and certainly what personality types are doomed to repeat heartaches still.

So many answers evade a clinical approach. Over and over for no obvious reason the most unlikely people are drawn to one another or sadly seemingly ideally suited people fail in friendship because one doesn't live up to the expectations of the other. Some people decades on after their first encounter could be said to have been bewitched in their friendship and seem to be delighted and surprised by each other speaking of the magic of their friendship and the transfiguring qualities of their union. These ideas are more than merely figures of speech. The possibility of magical friendships is there for everyone and rituals handed down through generations show how to meet, secure and enthral a friend. Some are playful, some funny, some poetic and some potent, and some require that we look inward to see if previous misfortune in friendship can be resolved by a simple change in approach. This could be to adopt a new positive attitude. Certainly there is a right state of mind for being cherished as a friend. This begins by being as modestly happy with oneself for if we don't love ourselves how can we expect anyone else to find us lovable. If we are riddled with self doubt and lack of confidence how can we expect to be relaxed enough to develop the friendship we attract in the first place?

Those considered lucky in friendship have a special spirit and sense of self worth which may make them more magnetic in a crowded room. When you find a potential friend it is often the case that you give off an enigmatic radiance that others are attracted to yet when you are bereft of friendship you emit a signal of insecurity, brittleness and desperation which makes others avoid you almost instinctively but this need not be. If something in our body language and psyche enables others to read and understand what we are looking for and if a room full of unfamiliar people responds to the signals we give out then we must learn how to make use of this in seeking friendship. We can heighten our awareness of what it is to keep a friendship happy and hopefully learn how to evolve the friendship to greater levels of closeness.

Chapter 12

Amy's Story

Amy was now forty one years old and happy with her life. She was woken by her mobile alerting her to a voicemail message and she could not imagine who would be calling so early. Bleary eyed, she retrieved the message and she was astonished and shocked to see 'Maisie wants to be friends'. Was it someone playing a cruel game because the message was from someone who was dead and had been dead for twenty five years. She felt sick and apprehensive and a whole lot of other emotions arose in her. The message she saw was Maisie saying what she had said all those years ago but that could not be. The dead cannot rise and Maisie had definitely died. She read the message over and over all morning trying to find some sense in it and becoming more troubled by it.

She paced up and down wondering what to do next. It must be someone's idea of a sick joke surely but who? Who could think this was funny? Who knows the effect it would have on her? Of course all she had to do was delete the message. A part of her was screaming out to do this to end it but another part, a quiet and buried part, wanted to know, to understand. Twenty five years ago she was a schoolgirl and that was when it all began, the day the new girl started – Maisie. It was the day the first one of the year when you could smell Spring in the air. Amy and her three friends were a close knit group. They were chatting and laughing in the sunshine and the sky was the most amazing blue. They were sort of shining too as they walked around in a group always together. The new girl's name was Maisie. She looked OK, not trendy but not square either. As Amy scanned the cafeteria trying to find her friends so she could sit with them, Maisie was sitting on her own at one end of the table. Amy caught Maisie's eye and asked her how her first day was going so far.

"It's different you know."

"So crap basically," Amy said.

"Yes," was the reply.

Amy asked her where she went to school before.

"My parents moved, we lived in London."

"It seems a funny time to move so near to the end of our last year."

"Yes I was having trouble with some of the other girls."

"Well everyone is nice here. We go into town after school. You should come."

"I can't today, my brother is picking me up, but I'd love to another day."

She told the group she had been talking to the new girl and asked her to come into town with us some time.

"No way. We have heard things about her, some stuff that happened at her old school."

"It's OK, she told me."

"Did she tell you what it was all about?"

"No."

"Well maybe you should get your facts right before you go inviting people out with other people."

"Anyway she can't come today, she is meeting her brother."

"Yes he is a bit of a weirdo, we've heard."

The group went off without her and she felt she had ruined everything. Maisie wanted to be friends with me and maybe that was the problem all along. She wanted to be friends with me and I had let her down. She had been hovering at the edge of her consciousness for all her adult life although she had been good at keeping her just a blurred shadow in the corner of her eye, lost but not quite out of sight. Maisie wants to be friends but she has been dead for twenty five years. Then Amy received another surprise jolt, an invitation to the yearly school's reunion. After all these years without anything and now this. Were the two things connected and why has it taken until now for her to be invited? Her neck was flushed and there were treacherous foolish tears prickling at the back of her eyes. How easily and how stupidly she was transported back through the years and how quickly that familiar feeling rushed over her. Shame at being left out and left behind, an afterthought. The wind outside was raging and she gets up and peers out but it is dark and she can't see much beyond her own reflection. A sudden rain shower rattles against the window as if someone had thrown a handful of gravel and she jumps back, her heart thumping. She recalled the group talking about the new girl.

"What do you actually know about her and where has she suddenly appeared from, all the things we have heard about goings on at her last school, but if you want to be friends with her Amy then of course that's up to you, but don't dump us your old friends otherwise you'll lose us, but obviously it's up to you who you are friends with, but if we were you we would think very carefully about where our loyalties lie."

Amy wondered whether she was ready to throw all that away for someone she could like but hardly knew, who could potentially end up being her only friend. The next day at lunch Amy was with her friends when Masie came up and asked to join them, looking at Amy and the empty seat.

One of them said, "Sorry that seat is taken."

"It doesn't look taken. It looks totally empty to me." She looked at Amy hoping for a smile or at least an acknowledgement but Amy did not even look up.

"We are saving the seat for a friend." The emphasis on friend couldn't have been more pointed.

"OK, I get the picture," she said and took her tray over to the furthest possible table. As they left the canteen Amy looked over at her. She thought of her now sitting on her own, her lunch barely touched in front of her, hunched over, a pale faced, sad person staring unseeing at a book. A week passed but Amy was struggling to concentrate on work and with every day that passed there was a tiny seed of hope that it had all been a joke, then there was a text message on her phone. It said, "Run as fast as you like Amy, but you will never escape from me, every wound leaves a scar." She sits for a while, heart racing, reading the message over and over again, seeing if it would yield some further clue as to who was doing this and why 'run as fast as you like'. Maisie had made a friend at school, a loner, Sheila, who she'd talked to in the last few months of the year before the leavers party. There were spaces, huge gaps in what Amy knew about Maisie and maybe Sheila might be able to fill them in. She typed Sheila's name into the computer and found that she was a solicitor living and working outside London. She picked up the phone now she knew where she worked and made an appointment giving a false name. She had a cancellation the next day so Amy made the appointment. She drove there and on arrival was buzzed in and asked to wait in the movies idea of an English law firm. A few minutes later she was shown in by an elegantly groomed secretary. Sheila raised her head with a welcoming smile but within a second it faded, her eyes registering shock. She waited for her secretary to leave before speaking and when she did her tone was blunt and unfriendly.

"Why are you here?"

"I didn't know where else to go."

Sheila raised an enquiring eyebrow. Amy told her she had received messages from Maisie and told her what they had said. Sheila was bewildered and said, "No that is not possible." Amy says that she knows it isn't but well it has happened and she wondered if she would know anything about it or could throw any light on it.

"Why would I know anything about it? I am not in the habit of sending messages from a long dead school friend."

Amy said she knows that but she was frightened and told her that she had received another message and showed it to her. ""What do you think it means?"

"It's obvious isn't it? Maisie and I both suffered at the hands of you bullies. Whoever is doing that knows that. I know you never bullied me but you dumped me and never spoke to me again, but I don't think there is any other word for what you and your little group did to Maisie, is there?"

Amy was hot with shame and says she knows she treated Maisie badly but now she can't believe that she could ever have behaved like that. She said she was a different person back then and barely a day goes by when she doesn't think about her but she can't change what she did and she wishes she could. The worst is that Sheila doesn't know what she did, not really. What she can't understand is why it's happening now twenty five years on. She asks her if she thinks it has anything to do with the upcoming reunion. Sheila had no idea about a reunion and Amy leaves with the firm intention of heading straight home, but walking back to her car she had the feeling she was being watched. Instead of going home she found herself driving to her old school and she didn't know why. As she parked up opposite the school entrance all the awful memories came flooding back of the terrible thing she had done. As she approached the school still thinking uneasily of her conversation with Sheila the landmarks started to mount up, the bus stop with the carpet of cigarette butts, the high fence that still ran the length of the playground, the notice board by the front gate with its tatty bits of paper advertising heaven knows what. The buildings were largely unchanged, the old part of the school still handsome with its Victorian red brick façade, the new building grey and blocky, the product of sixties architecture that once thought itself so terribly modern. She was planning to drive straight past and to take a quick look at the place but amongst the faded notes on the notice board that looked like they had been there since her time at the school, a garish poster demanded her attention. She slowed to try and read it but could just make out the rainbow coloured bubble writing, School Reunion Class of 1989. She braked sharply and swung over to the side of the road, parking haphazardly, half on and half off the pavement. She darted across the road swerving to avoid the traffic to read the poster from top to bottom, which promised a disco, pay bar and cold buffet, eighties tunes and old friends. She looked behind her, feeling weirdly guilty as if someone might see her. She returned to her car and sat for a few minutes staring over at the school, trying to get to grips with the emotions rumbling inside her. She is a completely different person now to the schoolgirl who came here every day for five years and yet she wondered whether that was true. There must be some core part of her that is the same. The girl who did those things she did then was her. She started the engine and pulled off and when she got to the end of the road she had the choice of turning to the left to head out of town or right towards the main residential part of town. She turned right, realising that the contours of the road have been saved somewhere in her brain, a muscle memory that still worked twenty five years on. Without thinking she took another right towards her old house. The street was still lined with identical 1970s houses. She carried on to re-join the main road at a different point but meeting a now one-way street, she had to detour and realised she was on the road where Maisie had lived and she pulled up outside the house, remembering the last time she had been here visiting without her group knowing. She got out of the car for some air before returning home. A bald man comes along pushing a baby in a baby buggy. As he passed her their eyes met and there was a moment of recognition before she gasps and he does a double take. A shard of ice slithered down her back. He looked older, older than his years in fact, but she would know him anywhere. It's Maisie's brother.

"Amy," he says standing still in the middle of the pavement, "what are you doing here?"

She says she is meeting a client. He looked at her dubiously. "Where?"

"Turner Street," thinking of her own old street.

"What do you do?"

She told him she had an interior design business. The unease which had been stirring inside her since hearing his voice steps up a notch. He asks her if she has heard about the reunion and whether she is going. She says she thought she might go sort of on Maisie's behalf. The mention of her name takes Amy's breath away and although she has occupied a private space in her mind for so long until recently, the past week she hadn't heard or spoken her name since she was a teenager. She thought she would get through this whole utterly strange conversation without talking about her. Suddenly she couldn't let the moment pass without at least trying to tell him how sorry she was.

She screwed up all her courage and said about Maisie. She is sorry she knows she treated her badly and she wished she could go back and change it. He looked away and said he didn't blame her and that no one knows what happened that night. He said he knew that Maisie was having trouble and Amy though that it was nice of him to phrase It like that but she knew the truth, they had made her life a misery. He says that no one else can take responsibility for what happened to her, either she bears that herself or it was an accident, a mishap or a once in a million chance. He watched her closely and Amy shifted from one foot to the other, wishing this encounter over and she wished for everything in her that his version of events was true. Of course it can't be and she wished she could tell someone the truth without being judged or worse. She wished that she could loosen the secret within her and untie a knot that is so tightly tied that no one could ever get its intricacies to tug it apart. He doesn't know it but they are talking at cross purposes. He thinks they are talking about the fact that she abandoned Maisie for the established group and the promise of popularity and how she was partly responsible for ostracising her at school. He thinks they are talking about a bit of schoolgirl bullying not sticks and stones but words that were meant to hurt and did and it is true she did all that. She had ignored her, deserted her and let her down. What he doesn't know is that she had also done something else, something much worse.

They say goodbye and Amy drives slowly back through the streets of her childhood. Then she remembered something he had said and that was Maisie is tougher than she seems, a slip of the tongue maybe or perhaps seeing her had thrown everything up in the air but there is no denying it, he had referred to Maisie in the present tense. Under the covers safe back home her thoughts take over. Some days she feels like a prisoner in her own home. There is no reason why she can't go out of course. Nobody could tell from simply looking at her but on days like today it feels as though someone has peeled back a layer of skin leaving her face redrawn offering no protection from the elements. From anything on these days she hides away until she feels able to face the world again, ready to put her mask back on to keep on smiling. She wonders sometimes how long she will be able to keep it up. Forever.

In some ways she is so used to keeping this secret that it comes naturally and on the days when it doesn't, when she yearns to open her heart, her mouth, to let it come spilling out, she can't keep quiet. Don't tell. The consequences would be worse for her than for anyone else. So she carries on shaking off those thoughts of the past that haunt her. She fears the present too some days as it's not only the past that scares her and not even staying at home helps. Sometimes she feels even more suffocated indoors than she does out in the world.

People are not to be trusted with her story. She does not need to be reminded that not everyone is not what they seem. She of all people knows that only too well. She pours a glass of wine and sits at the kitchen table, the lamp casting a calming glow and she checks her messages and each time there is not a message the faint hope that it is over grows and that it was a stupid prank someone was playing, a joke upsetting and disturbing, no more than that. Later on she checked her messages again, not expecting any, but she did it with trepidation and the message was from Maisie. It said, "Did you enjoy your trip? I haven't forgotten what you did. I am always watching you and I will never let it go." The blood drains from her face and she is overwhelmed by fear and there is the school reunion the next weekend and she thought she might go to see if anyone else had received such messages or knows anything about it.

The last time anyone had seen Maisie was at the end of school leavers party. She had wandered off to the cliffs and was never seen again. Her body was never found, the cliffs a bit like the suicide point at Beachy Head, depending on the tides whether bodes got washed up or not. The next thing was that she received a phone call from Sheila which surprised her, informing her that there was something she had not told her and she suggested a meeting and she said it was relevant to what was happening. They agreed to meet up in a pub in London and even today Amy thinks that there is something about London that gives her a thrill, not just the bright lights but the murkier depths too.

She walks through Soho absorbing the heavy scent of garlic and wine, chips and cigarettes, smoke, rubbish and drains. She felt alive, anonymous and part of something that counted, a heady mix of hen parties, work nights out and viveurs, sex workers and criminals. Soho like everywhere had changed. There were more restaurants, more toilets and less obvious grime. There were even more tourists. She wonders if she has changed too. She is not so open to change, having to be on her guard all the time. She has created this persona of stability and contentment. Her phone bleeps with another message. "You do not deserve to be happy, not after what you have done."

She stops stock still on the pavement, her legs almost giving way beneath her. It is noisy but all she can hear is her own panicked breathing and the beating of her own heart. Someone must be watching her and as she looks around the street is busy, filled with ordinary people. She scans their faces but there are too many of them and she doesn't know who she is looking for. It feels as though Maisie has crawled inside her head, her fingers reaching out and scraping her thoughts, taking the worst things she thinks about herself and serving them back to her. She keeps walking, staying on busy roads, avoiding the quieter side streets with their dark corners and shadowy wine soaked doorways, but even in the well lit people-thronged areas seem menacing because she doesn't know where the danger lies.

She doesn't know who she is frightened of or who she is running from. She goes to the agreed pub to meet Sheila who arrives on time. She once again tells her that she knows she treated Maisie badly, was awful to her and it was unforgivable and she wished she could change that but she can't, all she could do was acknowledge how wrong she was and says she is a different person now. Sheila says that she can understand that and says she can't arbitrarily think about our schooldays but thinking about those times she too is plunged back into it somehow. They stay with you, experiences like that, and although she is successful now she understands although there is still a part of her still hovering there looking in. Amy knows what she means because despite their different school experiences she feels that too. Sheila says that after the leavers party something was different, wasn't it?

Amy looked down and stares into her wine and says, not really but things were never the same. She is skirting too close to the truth here and she can feel it like an iceberg in the ocean at night. She doesn't know exactly where it is but she is so frightened of hitting it unexpectedly, of feeling it crashing down into her, tearing and splintering over her entirely. Part of her wanted to tell Sheila everything, to let her into the crushing fear that is consuming her. She wanted to shake her and make her hear that someone is watching her. Then she says that she saw Maisie's brother recently. Sheila says what was he like, fascinated as she always felt there was something weird about him and he was so protective about Maisie. Amy says that he seems to know an awful lot about her and Sheila too.

He knew what we both did for a living and she had got the sort of feeling that he had tabs on us both. Something else though, he spoke of Maisie in the present time. Sheila just stares, her face pale and there was an uneasy silence. Then she says that is what she wanted to talk to Amy about. Every year on her birthday she gets a present delivered through the post and it says every time "Happy Birthday Sheila, love from Maisie". Amy puts her glass down harder than she meant to, her hand jolting, threatening to spill it on the table. The chatter and buzz of the pub blurs, only Sheila's face is pinpoint sharp.

"Every year since school?"

"Yes."

She asks where they are posted from. Different places is the reply. Amy says, "You don't think it's from her, do you?" Her voice dropped to a whisper and the palms of her hands are painful realising that her nails are digging into her soft flesh. Sheila says that she has considered all the options and stopped trying to figure it out to be honest, but when Amy had shown up in her office she freaked out at the idea that Maisie was still alive, that the presents all these years were really from her. Amy sits back in her chair, her mind skittering about. It can't be possible that Maisie is still alive, and why is she the only one being persecuted. Is she being melodramatic thinking she was in danger. She can't escape the fact that she is being watched.

Sheila leaves and Amy is left to face her solitary journey home to an empty flat. She is worried that someone is following her. Sheila had seemed willing to forgive her for how she had treated Maisie, but Amy knew she would never forgive her if she knew the whole truth, not in a million years. Maisie's brother had always been protective. He knew what she had been through and knew her childhood and teenage years weren't exactly a bed of roses. He just wanted the rest of her life to be happy, that's all and he didn't want anyone else to hurt her, so the closer he kept her the safer she would be. Pre the leaving school party he had confronted Amy and told her to stay away from Maisie and angrily asked her if she had any idea what she had done. She wanted you to be her friend and you cut her down and she cut herself off from everyone because of the bullying from you and your so-called friends. You let her down and I hope you think it was worth it. Amy knew then that whatever she had with Maisie was well and truly over now.

There were no more chances to make amends. Back home she'd had the lights on all morning but they hadn't banished the Winter gloom, the rain lashing from a grey sky against the windows. All the week she had been putting off making the decision about the reunion and even now the day had arrived she doesn't understand why she kind of feels the need to go. No one knows how the school pulls her like a scar that itches, drawing fingers to it even though she should leave it alone to heal. Then another message, "Going back to the scene of the crime? I will be looking out for you." Each message is like a blow to the head from an unknown assailant leaving her reeling and confused and she knows it will never end until she confronts it. She doesn't know what this person wants but hiding here in her flat deleting messages is not going to solve anything. She thought back to the school leaving party and what they had done to Maisie. Maisie was devastated and Amy and her group had decided on one last humiliation for Maisie.

They had decided to grind up an ecstasy tablet and slip it into Maisie's drink so that the effect would put her out of control on the dance floor and everyone could have a good laugh. It fell to Amy to get the drug into the drink. Maisie had been sitting by herself with a glass of Cola, pale and alone. When she went to the toilet leaving her drink on the side it was the opportunity the girls were looking for and Amy slipped the powder into the drink while the others shielded her from any prying eyes. The deed done, they coupled up with the boys on the dance floor and became engrossed with the music. At the end of it Maisie had not been on the dance floor and was nowhere to be seen. Her brother came to take her home but she could not be found. The school was searched top to bottom and one girl said that Maisie had looked unwell and was seen walking unsteadily towards the cliffs. The police were called, the grounds and school were searched again and the cliff edge. Everyone was interviewed and Amy and her friends lied to the police, saying they had seen nothing as they were dancing all evening and had not seen Maisie at all.

The investigation following concluded that Maisie must have fallen or jumped off the cliff edge into the deep water beneath and would have certainly drowned. It was awful and Amy could never forgive herself for what she had done and twenty five years on she was still hiding from it. Keeping the truth within her all that day, reunion day, there is still a part of her that wonders if she is going to back out but a few hours later she is in the car dressed in a flattering black dress. She can't pretend any longer that she is not going to the reunion and she can't ignore the messages either and excitement runs through her at the thought of what or who is waiting for her at the school. She finds a space on the road opposite the school and thinks to herself that she could still turn back and just hole up at home but she gets out of the car and marches firmly to the entrance. She gives her name at the door and is given a name tag and walks into the lobby into the hall and it was the smell that hit her first.

Like all schools it smells of rubber and disinfectant with the hint of old sweat but the familiarity of this particular odour is like a smack in the face. It throws up memories she didn't know she had, queuing up for chocolate in the tuck shop, hot orange drinks from the vending machine, playtime as it was known then all now lost in the mists of time and of course another memory, another night in this hall, this one not lost but branded onto her brain an ugly scar. She tries to stem the images that were flashing through her mind and the accompanying wash of shame. With an anxiety bordering on panic little groups form and merge, people flitting from one cluster to another. She is the only one who has come without the security blanket of a friend or partner. She looks around she sees someone she knows and soon there are others she knows. The night wears on and the volume rises. There is laughter, there are the promised 80s tunes and bad dancing. The mood in the hall is a potent cocktail of nerve and excitement as the alcohol level in their collective blood stream rises and she could feel everyone slipping back into their teenage years and selves as if their personas were only something they were trying out for size.

In spite of an ever present watchfulness in her case she is actually having fun and she is now glad she came. Maybe this is what she needed. Exorcise those demons. The evening passes with nothing untoward and she goes home happy she had made the effort to go to the reunion. The following morning over breakfast she puts on the television news as she always does. The voice of the newsreader pierces the early morning and her words begin to make their way into her brain. "The dead body of a woman has been discovered by a dog walker in the woods behind a school outside London this morning. Police have not released the woman's name but it is thought she was attending a reunion at the school last night. They are asking anyone with any information to contact them as soon as possible." Amy was shocked, spilling her coffee on the counter top. It took her back to the night of the school leaving party hearing the words police and missing person.

The warm night had given way to a heavy Summer downpour, and then her father had collected her and then at home there was just a space and she had sat on her bedroom floor staring at it all night, a space where Maisie should have been dancing, going crazy, hugging people without knowing why and being watched by Amy and her group nudging each other and laughing, but Maisie had disappeared into this empty space leaving only the shadow of a scornful laugh, a wisp of smoke in the night air. That night was the end of everything and the beginning. The end of something is always the start of something else even if it can't be seen at the time. What did she remember? The heat of the day that lingered on into the evening, the ceaseless rain that followed, the earth beneath her feet solid and unyielding, the way she floated up above her body for a moment wondering what was going to happen next and it almost had nothing to do with her at all. Sometimes she doesn't know who she is any more. What she does know is the girl she was died that night and somebody else took her place. Ever since this new person has been scrabbling for a foothold, clinging onto the rock face, dirt under her fingernails. Like trying to breathe under water. There are very few people who knew about her old life in her new one, it's better that way. She avoids the awkward questions and changes the subject. She acts like she is a normal person just like everyone else when underneath her skin guilt and lies crawl like cockroaches.

When you leave something behind you think that's it, it's gone, but you can't leave yourself behind. This is it, this is you for life. She has been ignoring the past for a long time but she is beginning to wonder if she will be able to ignore it forever. It lives in her like a tumour or a parasite. Maybe it is time as they say to make sense of it, to wrench it out into the light, examine it and face it. Maybe it is only by going back that she will be able to move forward. Back to the television. The journalists haven't been given any information but the police want to talk to everyone who was at the reunion. They gave out a number to ring so she rings it and is asked to come in straightaway to an incident room they have set up in the school hall. She drives there, speaks to a policeman at the entrance and is told to go in. The hall looks different in the cold light of day. The disco, the debris and the banners are all gone.

A detective inspector asks her to sit down at the corner desk and chair and thanks her for coming in. He tells her that from a bag next to the victim identifies her and she gives Amy the name. It is her once best friend, one of their close knit group. The inspector asks if she knew her and Amy replies but says she hadn't seen her for over twenty five years as they hadn't kept in touch. She has an ache in her stomach which twists and grips. There comes a lot of questions to answer like when did she see her at the reunion, who did she speak to, was she with anyone and what time did she leave. She told the inspector that she was with a man she had apparently met online a short while ago and it looked like they had an argument towards the end of the evening not long before she last saw her.

"Do you know where we might find him," he asks.

"Sorry No, I only know his first name, James, and that he lives in London."

"OK," said the inspector, "we will want to speak to you again in due course but if there is nothing else you can think of, just one more thing, we found something near the body. Have you seen this before?"

"No," she tried to answer naturally.

"The victim wasn't wearing it?"

"No, she was wearing a big silver statement necklace."

Even though Amy hadn't seen it for twenty five years she would know it anywhere, it haunts her dreams. Without a shadow of a doubt that was Maisie's necklace and she wore it all the time and she was wearing it the night she disappeared. Back home she can't ignore the possibility that whoever killed her friend had also killed Maisie and she feels in danger. What if she is next? She wonders if she could throw off this dark heavy cloak of secrecy that she has been wearing, just put it down and walk away, because the person she should have been all along was not her now.

She has lived her life in shadow, running and hiding. Yet she can put a good face on it when she needs to but inside she is still that sixteen year old schoolgirl. She is torn between the gut twisting fear of anybody knowing who she really is and the contrasting desire to be truly seen. Isn't that what we all want really? She wants to step out into the light and live the life she should have lived. She wants to be heard. She wants to be know. She thought about Maisie and what had happened to her at her old school, so bad it seemed that the family had to up sticks and move. Apparently it was all because of a boy who was friendly to her but then he started to want more and told her he was in love with her but she told him she wasn't interested and just wanted to be friends but she felt uncomfortable around him and pulled back, starting to spend less time with him. That is when it started.

He began to send her notes saying they should be together and waiting for her outside her home, wanting to walk with her and when she wouldn't he would walk a few metres behind her all the way. Then when he was getting nowhere with that he ramped it up a bit , being outside the house at night looking up at her window, and then the rumours started, horrible stuff, sexual but not only that she had slept with such and such a boy but girls too. Girls started to avoid her even ones who had been her friends and boys who had never even noticed her started sniffing around and then a rumour went out that she had slept with three boys at once, one in each hole. He then wrote to her parents as a concerned well-wisher, telling them about the rumours and things that were being said about her, so they moved and hoped it would not come with her. It was awful.

It was all beginning to fall into place. The same person who killed her school friend had also killed Maisie, the necklace linked them. The investigation continued. Apparently her friend at the school leavers party had seen Maisie leaving the hall and followed her. She was stumbling and clutching her stomach down the path towards the wood and she was panicking and did not know what was happening. She tripped and fell at the cliff edge and then the figure of a boy appeared. He began stroking her and kissing her and then he lay on top of her and in spite of her drugged state she began wriggling, trying to get out from under him and he raped her.

As soon as he rolled off her she scrambled to her feet and staggered towards the school, saying she was going to tell everyone what he had done and she started shouting rape. He had to make her be silent so he grabbed her, pulling her necklace off and putting it in his pocket so that the body could not be identified by it later and he pushed her over the cliff edge and heard the splash as she hit the water and she was gone. The tides must have been his friend that night. Maisie is out there somewhere or what is left of her bones when they have been in the sea for twenty five years. At the reunion he had been seen in the shadows and he had seen that he had been watched and had a faint image of who it was who had seen him.

The years passed and he organised the reunion under a different name and armed with the research he had done over the years as to who it was. He knew of Amy's little group, the most popular girls in the school, and knew that they had bullied Maisie, hence the messages he had sent to them all apparently. He also sent the packages to Sheila, the only one who had befriended Maisie. At the reunion he stayed in the shadows observing and unseen, and he heard the girls talking about what they had done to Maisie. When Amy's friend went out for some air and a smoke he followed her and dragged her out to the woods knowing she was the one who had seen him with Maisie that night. With gloves on he strangled her and left her body in the undergrowth but on pulling his gloves out from his pocket Maisie's necklace had dropped on the ground and he hadn't seen it.

With the police all over the place now searching for Amy's friend and finding her with the help of a passing dog walker in the woods, he could not go back for it. The whole story eventually came out and the boy was jailed for life for the two murders. Amy had not been the one who had killed Maisie. Speaking to the police, Amy told them everything, and given the passage of time it was unlikely any action would be taken against her in relation to the death. Knowing that, she had paid a terrible price for the knowledge she had had but no more than she deserved. She thought of Maisie's last moments and her friend too. Finding the person responsible did not absolve her. She still did what she did to Maisie. She had played her part and she cannot atone for that and she cannot live her life, the rest of it, in the shadows. She has to move into the light and she can no longer let it define her, but she can learn from it and live a better life as a result. The wall around her had vanished and with that Sheila and Amy cultivated their friendship and became close friends.

Chapter 13

Theo And Janet's Story

Theo and Janet had been married for ten years. They had started out as close friends and were then best friends devoted to each other, were happy, successful and had built their entire life together around the common expectation that after passing thirty they would want to settle down and have children. By then they mutually anticipated they would have grown weary of their travels and would want to settle down and have children, would be happy to live in a big happy household full of children and homemade quilts with a garden in the back yard and live a normal happy ever after family. However she was appalled to be finding out not to be wanting any of those things. It was a cold dark night in December 3am in the morning.

Her husband whom she loved very much was sleeping in bed but she was hiding in the bathroom for consecutive nights and, just as all the nights, sobbing so hard in fact that a lake of tears was spreading before her on the bathroom tiles, a veritable lake of all her shame and fear and confusion. She doesn't want to be married any more and she was trying so hard not to know this but the truth kept insisting itself to her. She kept wanting to have a baby but it did not happen and she knew what it felt like to want something. She well knew what desire feels like but it was not there. How could she turn back now though? Everything was in place and this was the year but she was utterly consumed with dread.

What a catastrophe and how could she be such a jerk as to proceed so deep into her marriage only to leave it. They had bought this beautiful house which she had wanted and loved it, so why was she haunting its halls every night, now howling like Medea.

She was proud of all they had achieved, this prestigious home, also an apartment in the city, their friends, the parties, the picnics, the weekends roaming the aisles of the superstore together buying ever more appliances. She actively participated in every moment of the creation of this life so why did she now feel like none of it resembled her?

Why did she feel so overwhelmed with duty of being the housekeeper, part breadwinner, social organiser and coordinator, the dog walker, the wife and in her stolen moments a writer and it is not at all what she wants. Her husband was asleep and she loved him but she could not wake him to share in her distress and what would be the point? He had already been watching her behaving like a lunatic falling about for months and it only exhausted her and him. They both knew that there was something wrong with her and he was losing patience with her. They were weary in that way that only a couple whose marriage is collapsing can be weary and they had the eyes of refugees. Although she felt that her marriage was a failure she did still want to be his wife, all the wonderfulness and why she was unable to imagine life with him. It is sufficient to say that he was still her lighthouse and her albatross in equal measure.

The only thing more unthinkable than leaving was staying, and she did not want to destroy anything or anybody, she just wanted to slip out of the front door without causing any fuss or consequences and then not stop running. This part of her story is not a happy one and she shares it because something was about to happen on the bathroom floor that would change the progression of her life almost like one of those crazy astronomical super events like when a planet flips over in outer space for no reason whatever and its molten core shifts, relocating its poles and altering its shape radically, such that the whole mass of the planet suddenly becomes oblong instead of spherical or something like that. What happened was that she was begging for help, like to a higher being saying please tell me what to do over and over.

Seven months later she left her husband. This episode had had the hallmarks of a conversion experience, the dark night of the soul, the call for help, a sense of transformation. She believes that what happened between her and her husband was not the leaving but that they shocked each other by how swiftly they went from being the people who knew each other best in the world to being the most mutually incomprehensible strangers who ever lived. At the bottom of that strangeness was the abysmal fact that they were both doing something the other person would never have conceived possible. It was the very end of a best friend loving friendship, something they would never have dreamt would ever happen, but it did.

Chapter 14

Four Dimensions Of Friendship

The concept of friendship is historical. Philosophers in different cultures and epochs have emphasised certain aspects of friendship that others have not. In ancient Greece and Rome the civic dimension of friendship was prominent as some argued that it was part of a social glue that held societies together. By the seventeenth century however friendship's centrality for a good society began to be questioned when the possible socially destabilising nature of preferential love was challenged. Identifying the convergences and divergences in the philosophers' views of friendship is important for understanding its nuances and in doing so look at the four philosophical approaches and dimensions of friendship.

These writings reveal friendship's significance and how friends help each other when they are weak and struggling. The need to take friendship seriously as a model for all relationships based on how friends courageously pursue a common truth together also emerges. Western philosophy's analysis of the concept in the early dialogues leaves us with more questions than answers including the unchallenged assumption that friends share everything in common whilst in contrast another view offers several claims and insights supporting the relevance of friendship for a good life beginning with unequivocal praise for friendship stating without friends no one would choose to live.

Beyond this affirmation are useful friends, friends for pleasure and virtuous friends, this one being the best as this is a friendship where each person loves the other because of his or her good character and this relationship leads to mutual betterment through deep concerns for the friend's welfare. Continuous personal development plays an important role in living a good life and friends mutually aid each other to improve their characters, cultivate joy in life and flourish as human beings. In this way friendship is indispensable to a good life. This stands in stark contrast to contemporary views which portray friendships being mainly about hanging out together with little emphasis on personal growth while another view thinks friendship is a necessary component of life commenting that any person existing in solitude is either beast or god stating that when someone enters a period of life when he is unable to carry out needed activities without a friend he may quit life.

Besides the aid friends offer is the ability of friends to help nurture peace in our emotional lives and to encourage our good judgement. So friends help one another to become better, stronger people by reducing emotional stress, helping each other to work through difficult decisions and by doing things the friend cannot do. This reinforces the idea that friends mutually uplift one another, that without friendship people may languish under the burdens of life. In other words people have weaknesses and moments when they cannot succeed by themselves. Friends sustain each other through such moments and these strengths complement each other.

Another approach sees things differently via the types of friendship, romantic desiring love, love of neighbour, charity, affection in general and parental love directing our attention to love of neighbour as a foundation. It describes friendship as a type of love between two or more people standing shoulder to shoulder inspired by and pursuing the same truth as opposed to jealousy, friendship being open to more than one friend and indeed the more friends we have the more they bring out our singular gifts. Each friend is unique because each one can help others to improve in distinctive ways.

Instead of friendship isolating people from the rest of the world it can be described as taking each friend beyond the narrow lists of the self, their friendship grounded in their shared appreciation of a truth, yet this truth is always beyond their full grasp. Friends exist then in a process of appreciating and pursuing a common truth. It is more about the joy of sharing in this experience of pursuit with those we love than it is about the end goal. This would make the friendship process orientated whereby the friend's growth is nurtured through a shared activity with well matched values. Another view grounds friendship, elevating it into a model and goal for life.

With romantic love's difficulties and marriage failures is argued that a new relational goal is needed. No longer should it be romantic relationships grounded in marriage. This does not mean these relationships are insignificant or should be eliminated but they should grow out of friendship and be shaped by its values and orientations. Some associate friendship with fierce tenderness, the analysis includes a focus on embodiment which emphasises the physiological dimension of relationships and spirituality which emphasises deep interconnections with others in the world. Love which emphasises emotion and commitments and power which emphasises the strength to alter the world and others. This idea of friendships, a fierce tender side is important because friendship becomes political.

It is not simply between two people in isolation, instead friendship exceeds the private sphere and may be a vehicle through which social change is possible. Friends can unite and encourage each other to take a stand against injustices and to work for peace in the world. With friendship as a goal and the leading relational model to see life in a new way friendship is the lens through which we can examine and reimagine private and public relationships, professions and life. No matter what we are doing, the concept of friendship should play an important role in how we think and act. Each different approach to friendship highlights a different angle and has different priorities.

Character development and friendship's centrality for a life well lived are important. The pursuit of a common truth and the non jealous inclusivity of friendship are important, friends helping friends in challenging moments is crucial. Being both courageous and tender in friendship and using friendship as the relational model are crucial. By bringing these different emphases together friendship can be seen as a type of relationship dedicated to helping others cultivate their best selves, even when the odds may not be in their favour. Courageously with receptiveness and tender attentiveness friends uplift one another to overcome life's burdens. By using friendship as a new way for seeing, thinking about the world and acting in it, the various relationships in which we engage could be transformed.

Chapter 15

Friendship For Education

Western philosophers have enthusiastically praised friendship and a few intellectuals have raised doubts about it but friendship has inspired many who have esteemed its benefits especially the reciprocal commitment to nurture each friend's best self. Similar admiration is somewhat lacking today however and the marginalisation of the importance of good relationships within higher education complements this trend with current attempts to make colleges more business-like, reductive assessments, benefit analysis and data have taken centre stage.

Students are statistics expressed in the language of graduation rates and post graduation employment which become selling points to attract future students. This environment shapes relationships between the staff too. In a competitive market place faculty need data to justify their existence and critiques of other work, in person or in print often appear more combative than constructive. The point seems to be to win mental warfare and so gain a superior reputation. Quantity has overshadowed quality and higher education misses the mark by not engaging and encouraging the whole student and the whole educator as they strive to become their best self. It is time to rethink the teachers' role and their relationships with students and colleagues.

We should be embracing an educational framework grounded in a philosophy of friendship to nurture and sustain a more caring mutually supportive intellectual community and the tension outlined revolves around different ways of understanding education's role. From a monetary role perspective education is about job preparation and how to capture a portion of the market, but from a different angle education concerns the development of cultures of intellectual enquiry focused on personal development, integrity and utilising diverse fields of knowledge for human fulfilment. In today's contest, while many students find education worth the investment, just as many find college classrooms uninteresting. Campuses have high levels of student depression, anxiety, drug and alcohol abuse, assaults and racism. For professors the problems are just as real but of a different kind. Studies have found that professors are dissatisfied with their work and lack enthusiasm, and a scarcity of job security for more tenured staff has led to unhappiness, a lack of motivation and negative attitudes in the classroom. Shrinking departments, more responsibilities and less support have created a downhearted group of educational labourers. Academia then needs an alternative approach that can cultivate better relationships, improve environments for both learning and teaching, and develop more advantageous conditions for personal and social growth. A theory of education grounded in friendship is one response so we will focus on the relevance of four dimensions of friendship for higher education, and they could shift communities of learners' activity away from a monetary economy toward a focus on the talents and potential of individuals.

Chapter 16

Bringing Friendship Into Education

Taking friendship seriously in the educational environment means moving beyond contemporary ideas of education focused on employment, hyper-rationalism and rote learning. Instead friendship redirects attention to the relational dimensions of education placing relationships at the centre of learning environments. Whether between students, between teachers or between students and teachers, a friendship educational model emphasises how these relationships can be more open, mutually supportive and focused on nurturing the best in each person. It moves the focus away from quantification and reductive assessments, a monetary economy and unsupportive power dynamics, toward a focus on everybody's gifts and processes aimed at mutual betterment and greater relational equality.

A philosophy promoting friendship in higher education, to stay focused on people helping one another to grow, the relevance of the emotional life for education, the significance of a shared truth and a consensus of values and the need for courage and care in intellectual pursuits. This would help dispel the dejectedness permeating higher education through engagements that encourage the development of the whole person in a supportive community. Students pursue education to attain specific goals, self betterment, a financially secure job, their lifelong dreams, offers financial stability and allows them to pursue their dreams within and beyond classroom. But education expands beyond facts from a text book or exam successes, it concerns learning to live well in every realm of our lives and in every context as we enter or at least try our best to improve. A certain philosophical view of friendship reminds us that education is more than an instrumental good reminding us that there is more to think about than the pleasure and utility students and educators get from the classroom. Rather through nurturing friendship the classroom becomes the site of mutual support.

In seeing students and teachers through the lens of friendship the relationship becomes about mutual betterment making students better students and educators better educators and all of them better people who live more fully. The emphasis on friends being concerned with the excellence of their friends is crucial for rethinking education because it redirects attention to the cultivation of a good human being. Moreover this reorientation can affect every relationship the students and educators have whether on campus, in wider society or at home. Relationships in educational contexts occur with a lattice of lives with unique struggles, fears, joys and hopes.

Surface interactions however fail to go beyond polite pretences and habitual decency. Yet by understanding of friendship educational systems could learn to avoid the distancing effects of titles and power and dive below the surface to engage the challenges people face. Students and teachers could also learn from emphasis of friends helping one another with intellectual problems and decision making. The development of critical thinking skills is already a big part of education but their development could be greatly facilitated by emphasising friendship in educational relationships. Friendship's emotional side may seem inappropriate for student teacher relationships and unnecessary between colleagues.

The problematic assumption here is that emotions are unimportant in the educational environment except in extraordinary circumstances such as dealing with distraught students. Understanding of friendship emphasises cultivating the whole person, the rational and the emotional dimensions, to bring balance to lives and relationships. Instead of thinking about learning only as a rational process leading to intellectual autonomy, students, teachers and colleagues should acknowledge and honour the emotional depths of those with whom they relate. This provides an opportunity in education to encounter others through intimacy with their emotional worlds. Some philosophers focus on the open delight friends share with each other as they pursue a common truth or idea, each person bringing out different dimensions of their friends from actions and intellect to emotions and humour.

What is most important for the educational system and environment however is that friends are following a unique idea of truth. In educational friendships for example a common vision would be associated with social justice, diversity or living a good life and being a good citizen. Students and educators could bond in the classroom, in the halls, over food or in meeting in mutually supportive ways to understand a common truth. This creates commonalities among the members of the community, bringing people, their minds, intentions and actions together grounded in common values.

Despite differences students and educators stand shoulder to shoulder in an inclusive way. Such consensus in diversity supports character development and the expression of individuals' unique attributes, intellectual and emotional belonging and security with the campus community, stressing the importance of the example of friendship for all relationships, how no aspect of life can escape its relevance. Just so, the role of students and teacher should incorporate the values, support and benefits of friendship. An analysis forces us to reassess how mindful we are of the physical dimensions of education, students and academics are embodied beings. The focus also urges us to examine how love can shape and enhance educational relationships instead of competition and power hierarchies, love concerns aiding others to benefit and uplift them. Moreover incorporation and spirituality would mean that learning would transcend business models of reductionist views that self education solely for employment purposes.

Instead education would be grounded in insights into the endless interdependencies permeating both life and intellectual disciplines. Education, the multifarious aspects of life and the robust fields of thought should not be separated but woven together to bring multiple perspectives to bear on the complexities of existence. Finally strength or power in education means boldly pursuing learning, understanding the implication of thought and action and being able to choose the most beneficial paths despite resistance from unjust traditions. Pursuing friendship in education then does not imply making things easier and cosier. On the contrary education becomes more challenging and risky. Grounded in friendship values education would be concerned into changing people and the world through intrepid thinking that crosses boundaries and is sustained by courageous caring. Thus education becomes a process focused on healthy relationships uplifting all who take part. This is a shift to quality and its value could be assessed by observing the increased trust, benevolence, open mindedness, understanding and empathy that binds the community together.

Respect for others is exemplified in the best friendships. The ability to transform conflicts into better relationships is another marker of a healthy community. Employment opportunities and capturing the market would still be relevant of course but they would be relegated to being a by-product of the beneficial relationships from the foundation and the educational motivational institution that has chosen to be guided and reshaped by a philosophy of friendship. Through healthier communities more supportive interactions beside and beyond the classroom and deeper commitments to each other, colleges could gain reputations as transformative environments.

Chapter 17

Thoughts Re Education

There is little mystery concerning why philosophers have so highly revered the best in friendship as it is an open, caring relationship grounded in equality, mutual care and betterment, a deep commitment to each friend and an absence of the limitations found in other ways of loving.

It is important to remember that community depends on friendship and when there is enmity instead of friendship people will not even share the same path. So the warmth of friendship is a crucial part of a good life and a healthy society as it brings people together in a lasting way. Furthermore it can be argued that a deep philosophical engagement with others is also an act of friendship.

Philosophical pursuit takes on added significance when one remembers that philosophy's etymological roots are in the love of wisdom and philia.

Friendship has received more praise then disparagement from philosophers and this is because ideally friendship helps to bring out the best in people. It does this by being receptive to friends' unique gifts and enhancing them in ways that helps friends to become the best people they can be. In this way cultivating friendship can aid students and educators to focus on each other's gifts to help each person to develop in his or her unique ways and to do so in a caring, courageous and receptive fashion.

By putting friendship at the centre of higher education the classroom and the entire community could become more humane and focused on the various dimensions of every person's life.

Higher education is in dire need of help. Through nurturing

friendship education could become much more than it is and more able to honour and cultivate every community member's distinctive gifts.

Chapter 18

Friendship With God

Friendship is the ideal way we should relate to other thinking beings and we ought to be friends with those around us because this will enrich our lives in virtue. Philosophers see the good life as the virtuous life and we need friends to receive many of our acts of virtue. However some philosophers stretch the notion of friendship far beyond just having warm interactions with the rest of humanity and this centres on friendship with God, but that idea is problematic for many people.

It may strike some as an unreasonable ambition to become an acquaintance of the Almighty, particularly if one regards only friendships between equals as genuine friendship. Some will see the gulf between God and humans as immense and will question the view that we can befriend God. The difference in our status rules out any possibility of comradeship. We do not need to be comfortable with all aspects of an analysis to accept its conclusions.

Chapter 19

Thinking Ahead ... The Afterlife

In the analysis of friendship some philosophers look ahead to the afterlife when they hope they can live in the beautiful vision of paradise in which we enjoy the bliss of being in God's company together with the community of the blessed who have made it there too. So we should be friendly with fellow human beings now because in the future they may with us be friends with God. The principle is pretty much any friend of God's is a friend of mine. A further reason is that being friendly with everyone is simply the charitable thing to do but taken to mean generally benign disposition towards those we encounter. This is the guideline many people can probably accept.

It is a subject of the golden rule that most religious and secular codes contain. Treat others as you would like to be treated. If we would prefer to be treated in a benign and charitable way for the sake of consistency we ought to also to behave in that same way towards others. Charity can be defined in a way that sounds strange to modern ears as the friendship of man for God. A charitable attitude towards our fellow man is merely a secondary manifestation of this virtue. God is the primary focus. To be friends with God the supernatural virtue of charity is needed and this rubs off in our dealings with mere mortals.

Chapter 20

The Key Effects Of Friendship

Some philosophers promote humble friendships with fellow human beings as part of an overall belief system in a benign God who can also be our friend. People have a value completely unconnected to their social status and they have value just because they are made in the image of God and also have the potential to be a friend of their creator. That is the way of looking at friendship. It is only convincing to theists though and perhaps just the subject of those who do not find the notion of friendship with God too hubristic.

We can still accept the principle that we ought to be friendly to other people in a non proud way. We are nowadays interdependent in several respects. One of these dependencies relates to knowledge so if we only ever befriend people like ourselves our knowledge base will suffer from being too narrow. In surveying knowledge as in surveying terrain a wide baseline for triangulation is desirable. To widen it requires us to entertain the opinions of others across an expansive social, cultural, political, gender and ethnic landscape and our epistemic mission should be animated by a spirit of concord, a union of wills. This can act as an antidote to the echo chamber effect of only having friends real or virtual who share our opinions. As a bonus we can also experience the pleasure of enjoying a wide range of delights in the company of our varied friends. The three key effects of friendship whether human or divine are concordia, benevolent-good action, benevolentia and beneficentia. Concordia is a union of wills – benevolentia – good will and beneficentia – good action, and these aspects are philosophically interesting irrespective of our beliefs or not in friendship with God.

Chapter 21

Confucius On Friendship

You cannot be friends with God, his reasoning being is that friendship requires equality and the gods are vastly superior to us. The argument is plausible as it seems difficult or impossible to be friends with a boss, mentor or teacher in quite the same way as one is friends with one's peers and equals. Indeed we might say that friendships are distinctive precisely in being non hierarchical. If I am truly your friend what I am to you is exactly what you are to me. This thought has been supposed to cause trouble for the followers of Confucius. Confucius was China's most influential philosopher and philosophical tradition for well over two millennia. Its ethical teaching has at its centre several hierarchical relationships that were intrinsically bound up with forms of propriety including rituals.

The second most famous Confucius thinker Mencius identifies five cardinal relations four of which are clearly hierarchical, ruler and subject, father and son, old and young, husband and wife, and sees the latter as an unequal relationship. The odd relationship out is friendship. Friendship seems to fit badly with the Confucian idea of modelling human relationships on family bonds. One possible comparison which sees friends as having a bond like that between older and younger brother would not secure the symmetry we are looking for. Friendship is also anomalous among the cordial relations in lacking ritual prescriptions and being voluntary. You do not choose your father, your ruler, but you do choose your friends. Confucianism became the philosophical movement of China.

Confucius would also have some reason to think that friendships should be unequal because for him the purpose of friendship is the cultivation of virtue. It seems a natural thought that we should therefore befriend those more excellent than us so as to learn from them. Confucius insists on symmetry in true friendship advising that we do not have as a friend anyone who is not as good as you are. It's been argued that in the light of this latter rule, Confucius could never have made friends at all. His disciples were certainly dear to him when he openly grieves for one of them who has died but does that mean he was this disciple's friend? The answer is No, as Confucius is peerless and hence friendless. To assert that Confucius had friends would diminish him.

His relationship with his students was arguably more akin to a hierarchical familial one as above, shown by the fact that he refused and referred to them as his little masters or sons. In keeping with the equality of friendship Confucius identified trust as its distinctive attitude, whereas a familial relationship would be characterised by an asymmetrical virtue such as filial piety. Confucius would thus discourage parents from trying to befriend their children, a common trend in modern family life. Just as a father cannot be the teacher of his son because their relation is too intimate so being over familiar is no way to be familial, but how does one cultivate excellence by befriending someone who is equal? After all it would seem that one would have nothing to learn from one's moral peer at least not in the way Confucius describes, ie 'In strolling in the company of just two persons I am bound to find a teacher and identifying their strengths I follow them and identifying their weaknesses I reform myself accordingly." Instead it must somehow be that sharing with equal others in the excellent moral life, or at least in the persisting pursuit of virtue, is itself a spur to the good life or even a constitutive part of it.

Confucius seems to have been convinced that this is so. For one thing no less than other relationships friendship gives us an opportunity to exercise virtue. Confucius himself aimed to bring peace to the old, to have trust in my friends and to cherish the young, and in advising us on examining our own character he speaks of reflecting on whether we have always kept our word with our friends. Friendship is also a source of delight as is made clear in this line, "To have friends come from distant quarters, is this not a source of enjoyment?" He informs us that the word friend has a strong implication of like mindedness and may especially indicate the bonds between the students gathered around one master. This is a hint towards a deeper importance of friends namely that they are embodied and embarked with us upon a joint project of self cultivation. We do not improve morally by looking to friends as a model for imitation as we might with a superior. Rather our affection for them is based on a recognition that they share with us our greatest pursuit. Confucius occasionally complained about being unappreciated by the morally inept. This may come as a surprise but is simply the counterpart of the joy he took in associating with those who shared his values. Birds of a feather flock together they really do, ideally by taking wing towards the height of virtue. The bonds of friendship are virtuous.

Chapter 22

The Friendship Between Philosophy And Science

There has always been much discussion about this category of friendship and at the very least it is a contentious issue between philosophers and scientists and on the face of it, it does seem an unlikely alliance but an interesting one which warrants investigation and a more in-depth discussion from both parties. Keeping an open mind ... some scientists say that philosophy is irrelevant, little more than esoteric, while some philosophers criticise scientism, the conviction that only science can be the source for all human knowledge, that all truth claims, all metaphysical beliefs should not only be informed by or founded on but entirely determined by empirical evidence.

So why does science need philosophy? Scientific verifiable facts about human beings should inform our ethics, the best system of ethics is a naturalistic system. Looking outwards to the world provides the raw material for any system of thought. After all philosophers point out that all knowledge begins with the information we receive through our senses. There is no reason to think that we could think at all if we have never heard, seen, felt, tasted or smelt anything to think about. It is thinking that allows us to achieve more than just sensing the world would end and the philosophy is the human species way of taking the art of thinking as far as it can go.

In doing philosophy we examine what the information we receive through our senses might mean in a larger context and in a deeper way. We question, we look for answers relentlessly not only because we want to solve problems but because we love to do so. Philosophy after all means love of wisdom and so we ask and as we look at the interplay between the input of our senses and the organisation of information through our thoughts, science then affords reality the opportunity to answer us back. Philosophy not only provides the impetus and the direction for scientific enquiry but once we find out the facts it helps us figure out what to make of them.

At every step of the way from the application of the rules of logic to the justification of why we should value or emphasise one set of facts over another in any specific application, the formulation of scientific theories relies heavily on philosophy. In fact science was originally a branch of philosophy, natural philosophy, until that branch of enquiry became so large it specialised and branched off again into physics, biology, chemistry and so forth. We could say that science was grafted out of philosophy. Those areas of philosophy that did not branch off into the sciences remained as the philosophical subspecies of metaphysical science, epistemology, ethics and so forth pursued largely behind the walls of academia today.

Philosophy is not limited to being an arcane, highly abstract field of enquiry, fascinating as that can be. Instead it is symptomatic of an approach to life for a perceiving, emoting, responding, loving, feeling, suffering and thinking being which approaches every person who partakes into one level or another. Philosophers want to know why and how and who and so on and not only to know what is but why we care about it and why others should too. Philosophers and philosophy from the very beginning originates in the public square. It is welcoming into one's self the whole world of things to sense and to imagine with a curious, critical attitude and engaging in that way of thinking with others. Science forms a big part of this but philosophy is prior to this and necessary for science.

To separate philosophy from science is as unhelpful as divorcing the individual from the species. One does not function without the other. When it comes to understanding the universe there is no such thing as non overlapping of magisteries of thought. Therefore it is a mistake to indulge in the kind of turf wars that science and philosophy sometimes have, not only because it sets up mental road blocks incorporating the full range of evidence and ideas available but also because it sets a bad example for critical thinking.

Chapter 23

A Co-Dependent Friendship

We would do well to remind philosophers, many of whom are remiss in this, that they need science to keep them honest, so that subtle errors in logic and justification and an over-weddedness to a tradition of thought cannot lead them too far astray. However philosophy critics also make a mistake when forgetting how much science owes philosophy and how heavily the scientific societies and scientists themselves actually depend upon it.

Some refer to the rights theory in philosophy as a popular source of ethics as a contrast to a scientific view referring to natural rights, part of rights theory, as a scientific ethical principle. Moreover like ethics in general, rights theory has always been derived if indirectly at times from the application of reason to observed facts about human beings that weave rational and feeling creatures, that we are capable of autonomous will, that we seek to live the good life and so on. To intimate that rights theory is or ever has been a non empirical view of ethics and an alternative to an empirical view is to misunderstand what rights theory is and always has been.

The ancient philosophers were founders of the most influential fields of philosophy ethics and natural philosophy better known today as science. They looked to the world to provide the raw material with which to craft their theories. It was their philosophical minds that drove them to ask questions and look for answers and it was nature that provided the subjects of their reasoning.

We can see from the accounts of the birth of science the beginning of a beautiful friendship between science and philosophy. The most intimate kind of friendship where the dialogue is open and honest and each supports the other, guiding one another from the pitfalls and wrong turns the other does not see. From the very beginning philosophy has always been there to keep science intellectually honest, supplying the discipline of logic and helping it to avoid methodological errors and how science can be used to help not harm.

Philosophy also makes it clear why there are relatively few direct or easy links from the factual is to the ought when formulating principles of ethics. It shows science that finding out how things work does not readily indicate how we should apply that information in our lives and that even the best scientist is prone to bias, misunderstanding and underestimation of that which we don't yet know. There is no honest philosophy without science but there is no science at all without philosophy.

Chapter 24

Friendship With Self

Philosophers regard friendship with self as one of the most important of all friendships. Every philosopher has a private notebook ready to hand at all times when they do not know what to do or need to talk or solve a problem, rise from a situation or require clarity of thought. Open it up to the first blank page and here recommences the most secret conversation, here in this most private notebook is where to talk to oneself and talk to the same voice one hears back their own and with training over the years found that voice again and learnt that the best way to reach it is in written conversation.

It is always surprising to find that accessing that voice is relatively easy. Even during suffering that calm compassionate affectionate and infinitively calm voice who is you the writer or maybe not exactly you is always available for a conversation on paper at any time of day or night. Hearing the voice, conversing with yourself on paper does not mean you are a schizophrenic, maybe the voice heard is your highest self or maybe it is indeed just a construct of the subconscious inverted in order to protect from inner torment or confusion. The saints of the day called such internal voice 'locutions' words from the supernatural that enter the mind spontaneously translated into your own language to offer consolation. The psychoanalyst would have said about such consolations of course that they are irrational and deserve no trust.

Experience teaches us that the world is no childsplay but the very fact that this world is so challenging is exactly why we sometimes must reach out of its jurisdiction for help appealing to our highest self or higher authority in order to find our comfort. At the beginning of this finding of our inner voice experiment I myself did not have faith in my internal voice of wisdom and that just takes time to perfect and I remember reaching for my private notebook and scrawling a message for my inner voice and my interior comfort in capital letters saying that I did not believe in you. But after a moment still breathing heavily came a clear pinpoint of light ignite within me and found myself writing an amused and ever calm reply as to who are you talking to then and have not doubted its existence again since.

In response somewhere within me rises now a familiar presence offering me all the certainties always wished for and what I wished another person would say to me when I needed them to. This strange interior gesture of friendship, the lending of a hand from me to myself when nobody else is around I am reminded that I recognise myself as a friend. Most people would not accept self as a friend so easy to acknowledge or accept but within the world of philosophy it is important, not at all strange and a vital friendship to have.

Chapter 25

Cultivating Friendship – How Should We Live?

This is a central human question because if we are to live a considered life we cannot but reflect that we are not alone. From birth through our upbringing our existence has been shaped not just by our own experiences and thinking but by our interaction with the lives of others most closely with family where we are constantly reminded of the continuum of a network of relationships.

Our sense of ourselves and our own place in the world is tempered by our awareness of others, of the lives they lead, their thoughts and feelings and our concern to lead a good life is therefore not solely about ourselves but embedded in our concern for others. In the process of trial and error which characterises our existence we seek to learn, to develop our understanding but we do so in a continuous dialogue, refining our beliefs and attitudes, being assertive when required attentive to alternatives, tolerant of misunderstandings and changing when necessary.

As we explore the richness of human life. We travel hopefully with the expectation that a sensitive, thoughtful and peaceable approach brings abundant rewards. Our ambition for a full and complete life lies not in the accumulation of material wealth much as we can enjoy the comforts of civilisation but rather in the quality of experiences and relationships that arrive in friendship and love. If we can live more in line with our needs, as against indulging our wants and if our style of living is more attuned to a sustainable environment then we can better resist the temptations of greed and selfishness which threaten human civilisation.

As we work to live as simply as we can in a complex world we can sit more lightly on the earth and influence others to do the same. If we mix optimism with realism we can do good in small measures, modest but worthwhile. Decades of crafting this pursuit of living and loving we will have some perspective on both faith and reason. Years of ordained acting out the faith will give reason to claim and make us adamant about heartfelt adherence to friendship and undaunted faithfulness to rational discipline. We will be convinced that we should use our heads and live from our hearts so with intention we would live a reasonable faithful life formed and influenced by a faithfully reasonable self-understanding.

So how should we live and how do we live are not necessarily the same but having aspirations and trying to live up to them is a good starting point. So the following is how we aspire to live. The most important point is that no one lives in isolation. From our earliest experiences we interact with others and the quality of our lives is largely dependent on that interaction. Beyond this everyone seeks happiness and in modern western societies this universal goal is taken for granted. The unexamined life as philosophers say is not worth living.

A thoughtful analysis of that coda when applied to each of our lives reveals that we usually only examine our lives when we fail. The corollary to this is therefore that a life without failure is a life not worth living and this is how wisdom evolves over a life's experiences not through success or study but through dealing with life's trials and tribulations. This is reflected in virtually every story told how the protagonist deals with adversity be it physical or psychological or both and this is why story telling is universally appealing. So should we live our lives by realising that every interaction in our lives is an opportunity to make our lives more rewarding by making someone4 else's life more rewarding? In any relationship familial, work, contractual or whatever either both parties are satisfied or both are dissatisfied.

It is very rare that we receive happiness at others' expense. An old Chinese saying, "If one wants to know the true worth of a person, observe the effects they have on other people's lives." It's not about our own achievements it is about enabling others to realise their own achievements. We would broaden the question of how should each of us live for although each of us is unique I believe we have a common human nature with common wants and needs. I believe each of us seeks happiness by which I mean a more or less persistent state of general physical, mental and emotional wellbeing characterised by enjoyment of life and we should enjoy living but happiness is attained not by pursuing it directly but through activities that bring it about.

These activities differ from person to person and one requirement then for happiness is had by individuals but we are social animals and so we can achieve it only within society and this means being moral. We must behave in ways acceptable to others and the first requirement here is to do no harm. Other will not accept harm to themselves and will harm you back. Next we should always try to be just to everyone for we want justice for ourselves so do no harm and be just are both subsumed in the maxim, "Do unto others as you would have them do to you." These sorts of maxims of duty are fundamental for a society of co-operative people which is required for happiness.

We can always avoid unnecessary deliberate harm to all others and we can always act with the intention of justice to everyone if we understand what justice requires. Beyond duty is love and love is wanting another to be happy and it naturally motivates our doing good for others. We can fulfil our duty to everyone but we cannot help everyone as we do not have the capacity to do so. Humanity should live in a way that helps everyone achieve the goal of happiness. The avoidance of pain needs to be taken into account when pursuing happiness as achieving one's happiness may have the consequences of causing suffering for another human being.

To help people make informed choices and decisions in life we must evaluate a choice by evaluating calculating the degree to which any given action will increase the overall sum of happiness and we also need to take into account the duration of the happiness that an action will produce and also acknowledge the pain that may result from it. However living a happy life does not mean a life of over indulgence any more than it means the other extreme of abstaining from actions or friendships that provide happiness or promote it. To seek happiness in a balanced way which would fulfil our basic functions as human beings. To find balance between our various emotions, behaviours and attitudes is how we should live. This way of living involves balancing our deficiencies with the over excess of the opposites eg shyness and vanity. With these ideas in mind it is possible to make informed and suitable decisions that promote joy in friendships. Most of us want to live well but we are often mistaken about how to do so. For example the drug addict who believes he is as happy as he can be is mistaken and will later acknowledge his mistakes, when with friendship from others he cleans up and the neurotic who constantly worries about things outside of his control is not living well without support of friends even if he believes he is.

However we have a nature that defines the real parameters for a flourishing life happiness friendship and goodness are not the result of arbitrary choices rather they arise when we actualise our natures so how should we live? To live well we need wisdom and friendships so we can learn to distinguish between what is in our control and what is not and so avoid investing our hope in what is not in our control. We can learn stillness from others and realise the interconnectedness of all things and we can learn the way of being instead of having.

Empathy and community and friendship grow from these insights which in turn nourish some of the deepest forms of happiness and human actualisation. We learn how to avoid vain desires and to not give in to emotions that create them, and so we learn to live a simple and meaningful life built around friendships clean living and reflection. We learn to use persistent enquiry which leads to humility and wisdom to provide was to cultivate health and virtue where health is the harmony of the body and virtue is the harmony of the mind. From friendships we learn moderation and how to cultivate virtuous habits. These are a taste for the wisdom found in philosophy.

How can we treat everyone as an end in themselves? We come to realise that the world is too vast for one brain to comprehend. In our globally interconnected worlds we are aware of only a fraction of the friends involved in our lives, the rest go unseen as means in our lives. Facing the world with our emotions and an open mind happy that this helps us to make the best decisions we can make

Shirley Hughes

knowing that just because someone sees the world differently to us does not main that they are not aiming for a good life too. Be happy, be kind to others and make a difference, cultivate friendships, value friends and remember everyone sees what you appear to be, few experience what you really are.

Chapter 26

Friendship Cards

We were never intended to walk alone in life and through life. That is why friendship was created and it seems like special people are placed in our path to walk with us. When two people have been friends for a long time their hearts are interlocked and what they are together makes them stronger. Together they tried their wings, soared high, crashed, celebrated and cried. They have dried each other's tears and picked up the pieces of broken dreams and together they have made things better than they were before. It is not even so much the help they have given each other, it is the absolute confidence that they are always there for each other, wanting, willing and ready to help. Above all friendship is a gift of one's self to another. They thank each other for sharing such a beautiful gift. There are friendship cards to say this.

Chapter 27

The Idea of Friendship – The Good Life

An important feature of the good life according to philosophy involves a concern for others. To show why this is so we examine the idea of friendship. We distinguish genuine friendship from the superficially similar kinds of acquaintanceship one in which the basis of the friendship is pleasure, the other in which is mutual usefulness and these shallow forms of friendship last only as long as the pleasure or utility they afford whereas true friendship lasts because it is grounded in good in the sense that one wishes for one's friend what is best for him. This friendship we call perfected because its good lies wholly within the relationship itself and does not treat it as merely instrumental for some other further end.

A friend is another self meaning that the kind of concern one has for one's own good is extended to one's friend too. Proper self concern is appropriate for an ethical individual who will be motivated thereby to act nobly and to make intelligent decisions about how to choose an act and who will therefore always see a social being and what is best for himself is at one with what is best for his friends and ultimately community. Thus to treat a friend as another self is always to wish the best for him for his own sake and to act accordingly.

The ideal of friendship is personal and mutual and involves sharing activities, discussing decision and actions and is co-operating and supporting one another. Because a friend is another self everything that benefits him in these activities will benefit one's self and the capacities and possibilities of each as rational agents will be enhanced thereby and the fullest development of each individual therefore requires friendship and all that it brings in the way of growth and realisation of moral character for all parties to it. In conclusion what is best and pleasantest for each creature is what intimately belongs to it. In applying that rule to man we see that the life of the intellect more than anything else is the man, and so the life of the intellect will be the happiest life for man. So what of the two important social values of justice and friendship. Justice serves the best interests of everyone's pleasure as a form of contract between members of a community to ensure that they do not harm or disadvantage one another.

Each individual stands to gain from such an arrangement and therefore it contributes to the pleasure of each. Friendship is quite a different matter as unlike justice it is not just an instrumental good but has intrinsic value being in itself one of the supreme pleasures. Its pleasure derives not only from what friends can do for each other and give to each other but in disinterested and altruistic actions. Unquestionably though there is a tension between the egoism that lies at the basis of this view and the great importance attached to friendship and the pleasure of altruism. However it is not resolved by jettisoning the idea that friendship is along the highest of goods. What is good? The answer can only be the considered life, free, creative, informed and chosen, a life of achievement and fulfilment, of pleasure and understanding of love and friendship, in short the best human life in a human world humanely lived.

Chapter 28

Sharing The Spotlight

Philosopher and photographer share their spotlight together … a special friendship as they share the fundamental acknowledgement that sharing constitutes each of us, that our being in the world is always already a being with, referred as our being in common. When we engage in acts of sharing we expose ourselves to each other and to the other. To be exposed means to be exposed in exteriority or to be in a relationship with the outside. Although from very different worlds the philosopher shares his thoughts and truths and the photographer his graphic powers. They shed some light and darkness on each other in their operation and compliance.

The photographer in an act of sharing opens up a space of communication when we are exposed to the camera lens. The philosopher opens up an emotional connection that is posed at the border of the sharing and the splitting of singular beings referred to as portage meaning both to share and divide. The photographer exposes community to itself, giving community the proofs of its sharing and the completeness of its sharing. The philosopher says that the photography lets the singular outline of our being in common and exposes itself.

The bringing together of the photographer and the philosopher in his thinking involves an act of coupling and as from the photographer's perspective the approach to photography raises the question of community by interrogating its very limits and possibilities of sharing. For the philosopher it's about trying to feel what the other person is feeling and how far can the so-called insider position go in the direction of the other person. It comes up against its limit so that each sharing never seems to be close enough. Freed identity and such a practice poses and exposes the space of limitability between the inside and outside and from the photographer and the photographic point of view it both shares and splits it.

Chapter 29

Philosophy Is The Friend of Wisdom

The word philosophy means the love of wisdom and wisdom is the possession of knowledge, experiences and good judgement. Yet knowledge itself is only information whereas wisdom is the use of knowledge to pursue the good life. Philosophy developed historically as a response to life in its broadest sense and so is a friend of wisdom only when it relates to and affects how we live. When we look at contemporary philosophy we are struck by a number of features.

Firstly philosophy is now not merely an activity it is a discipline which exists primarily within universities and share only texts which take a disciplinary approach and will be deemed worthy of evaluation. Central to disciplinary philosophy is that it does not respond primarily to any normal or social phenomena but instead sees everything through the lens of previous canonical works and seeks to move the thinking in canonical works forward in some way. Instead of the mind and the senses ranging freely over all phenomena in search of wisdom a very narrow concentration on the texts is demanded and these texts for the most part are very sophisticated.

Developing their ideas is usually accomplished by elaborating on their arguments. After a certain point increases in sophistication come at the cost of a ruthless narrowing of vision and it is impossible for any activity so constrained to retain a supple, open minded approach to wisdom. Professional philosophy has now attained such Byzantine complexity as to become a sluggish and immobile behemoth that waddles clumsily through contemporary life and only with the greatest difficulty catches a glimpse of any novelty out of its small bleary eyes. To return to the possibility of a comprehensive view of our circumstances and our world we need to jettison the academic ideal of the theoretical sophistication. Sophistication is not wisdom and on the contrary the harsh truth is that the advances in theoretical sophistication in philosophy and other humanities have rendered them less fit for their purpose of exploring, articulating and promoting the good life.

In order to be totally and truly philosophical that is to truly love wisdom one needs openness to experience and to the specificities of each new situation more than one needs any theory whatsoever. If becoming wise involves making effective choices that lead to a morally improved life it should then follow that philosophy that rational search for wisdom becomes its chief means of acquisition. By studying to be wise perhaps by reflecting upon the experiences of others or reading philosophy books we can improve our understanding of the world around us. This could make it easier to handle life's many challenges for example when it comes to distinguishing between our individual rights and our moral obligation.

Wisdom offers an objective that is more helpful than our own narrow selfish interests. There should be no mistaking wisdom for mere opinion, prejudice, bias or whim because true wisdom is consistently right and not subject to contradictions or change. Seeking to make wise choices is the closest we mortals can get to attaining the ideal order for living a trouble free life that allows us to do the right thing. Yet desiring wisdom as opposed to accepting folly can make us strongly vulnerable to the wily power of our own conceit in thinking that it is readily available for the taking.

Desiring to make consistently wise choices does not always mean that we will. Sadly many of us only discover the critical pearls of wisdom after we have royally screwed up. Life must be lived forwards but it can only be understood backwards. This recognition in itself may be the best opportunity for wisdom available to us. Methods of critically examining our ideas would make our pursuit of wisdom easier by helping us recognise and resolve ethical issues as they occur. Asking ourselves difficult questions about motives and means equips us to become more aware as to where flaws may occur in our often too easily formed assumptions. By careful examination we hope we can acquire a more complete awareness of what is required to act wisely.

Where this bogs down too often is in an inability to attain more than a mere checklist to what is subjective or moral in our lives. Maybe the time has come to return to the basics of the philosophical method to recognise how unwise we are in our struggle to be wise. Wisdom is understanding the fundamental nature of reality, life and humanity and using that understanding to guide our lives. Philosophy is the love of wisdom and so should be its friend. Now at best it is the friendly acquaintance. To be a friend of someone is to think of him or her often but you can read book after book on philosophy and find no mention of wisdom. A friend is helpful but philosophy today contributes very little to wisdom.

Even educated people rarely turn to philosophy for wisdom so how did this happen? Firstly the scientific revolution resulted in many disciplines of philosophy shutting off from it beginning with the natural sciences. Psychology is the most recent to do so and today many people go to psychology popular though it is for wisdom. They do this rather than to philosophy. The natural and social sciences do not provide wisdom for they look external to ourselves and our fundamental being can only be understood for within ourselves most importantly the sciences deal with fact but not value and thus even with the split off of the sciences there is still a role for philosophy and the role is to provide the understanding we call wisdom.

Secondly philosophy is divided into the analytic philosophy of the English speaking world and the varieties of continental philosophy. Analytic philosophy is fractured even within itself as it concerns itself with specific small problems. Its virtues are clarity and rigour. Its vice is the lack of a comprehensive view and hence any hope of wisdom. Continental philosophy has the virtue of seeing the goal of wisdom and hence of philosophy not just to understand but to act. It has a comprehensive view and the hope of wisdom but unfortunately it has the view of obscurity and esotericism but perhaps one day the analytic and continental philosophies will merge and philosophy will again be the friend of

Philosophy of Friendship

wisdom. Since the word philosophy and philosopher can be roughly translated as friend of wisdom we could easily assume that because philosophers were already once considered such, philosophy still has the friendship of wisdom and if not philosophy what then?

Some might claim that science has now replaced it just as mathematics has seemingly been shown to understand the universe better than theology so science it is alleged understands the everyday world even our political and ethical lives better than philosophy. However the death of philosophy although welcomed by certain scientists is not necessarily to their advantage. Despite the impact of science on the modern world religious extremism and other excessive and irrational modes of thought such as racism appear to be on the rise globally influencing much current opinion. By promoting uncritical beliefs and intolerance over critical reasoning these modes of thought are at best anti philosophy and anti science. Therefore applauding the demise of philosophy might be mistaken even for scientists.

It is easy to consider philosophy as presently stuck somewhere between scientific understanding and the irrationality of current social and political dogmatism, but this is not necessarily a bad place for it. Providing a buffer between their different modes of thinking engendering debate between the different camps and testing and evaluating the false certainties ambiguities and dogmas of every side philosophy can still have a place in contemporary thought. Philosophy has been referred to by some as a constantly assailed no man's land between science and religion. However a more accurate metaphor would be to think of philosophy as the fault line between the continental plates of knowledge and of philosophical debate as the tectonic activity, the earthquakes, volcanos created as these plates collide.

As long as the fault lines exist philosophical debate will continue and philosophy will still be one of the friends of wisdom. When wisdom is the goal of man the hammer of philosophy is to crack, destroy and deconstruct the dark deceptions of reality be it truth, suffering life or death let the analytic hammer fall lest self deceit or mad despair causes men's flourishing to stall for faith and nihilism come undone. With mighty will to power out of the abyss of meaninglessness makes self affirming flows. Just look how sweet the garden grows atop the lawn of wisdom's dawn when from on high the great minds cry within the existential thunderstorms who else can lead us through the dark on that lonely embark? They alone battle gods and monsters exorcise false diversions elevate true enlightenment, defile man's perversions.

Artists merely decorate, scientists merely gaze, poets radiantly elucidate in elegant turn of phrase but wisdom needs the philosopher's axe to steer and spear the being here. A compass, weapon, and learned master teaches us well, how not to fear and only through a love of fate can we create a life of meaning, value, beauty helping us embrace the night in gallant authenticity. In cavern's days the answer sleeps in misty mountain lonely star and so we try to unite truth. Approaching knowledge near and far yet the greatest minds to set us free are the ones who question why. If wisdom be no friend of philosophy who else will light the drear sky and vanquish life's futility? Philosophy is more than a friend of wisdom. Philosophy and wisdom are inextricably bound to each other. Wisdom was always understood and the real world as coming to understand one's own life, the lives of others and the relationship amongst us and more simply in befriending wisdom is the power to choose well.

Practical wisdom impels us to act in the right, good or just way or as good sense but in the service of good will also thought of as prudence, looking forwards and backwards before making a decision about whether and how to act. Wisdom involves the domains of rational decision making social behaviours involving empathy, compassion and altruism, self reflection, decisiveness in the face of uncertainty and tolerance of divergent value systems. So wisdom in its fullest senses of encapsulating knowledge, meaning and truth is necessary for a system to be encapsulated. Philosophy meanwhile arguably is the summation of our value systems as human beings and concerns all that is significant and or which matter.

The aim of philosophy has been given as to find a way of thinking better and as the study of reasoning about how we ought to act and as nothing else but the study of wisdom and truth in turn leading to calm and a serenity of mind, a greater clarity. Philosophy has also been characterised not as a body of doctrine but as an activity and by phenomenology as an optic, a way of seeing things. Philosophers have been described as lovers of the vision of truth and it is a matter not just of knowing but of understanding the meaning and the principles of knowing, rigorously putting concepts and ideas into perspectives so we can see that philosophy and wisdom are necessarily intertwined. They complete each other's existence.

Humans are unique in their ability to do philosophy to search for truth in order to obtain wisdom. However without paradoxically lies there is no truth. When we stop speaking about lies instead of talking of alternative facts or alternative truths we kill truth and get a glimpse of post truth, the belief in what we feel to be true, the quality of preferring concepts or facts one wishes to be true to those known to be true. In the post modern world each has his or her own truths and truth becomes just a matter of taste because we trust our guts instead of the facts. In fact though post-modern truth does not mask lies as truth is about renouncing both truth and lies.

The triumph of post-modern truth is our collective defeat of wisdom but the forgotten one and like an old friend waiting to be remembered philosophy awaits us to continue the search for truth so that lie does not lose its meaning. It is up to us, not only in the media, academia and in art but also in the streets to keep searching for truth and thus to keep truth alive. Truth is kept and held captive by envy, hypocrisy and stupidity but it can be rescued by time so maybe it is time for us to remember about philosophy the forgotten friend of wisdom as the hope remains that the search for truth can bring us together not simply as man but as humans.

Wisdom tipped her head beneath the lintel and twisted her shoulders through the doorway somehow managing to squeeze into the coffee house. She was tall and her shoulders were broad. It was hard to see how it was possible but she was dwarfed by the bag that she carried over her shoulder. She sat at the table with knees that peaked over the table top and ordered her expresso. The long and out of place sword that hung from her belt scraped across the floor in harmony with the chair legs as she settled herself into a more comfortable position. She had been out on the plains of science stuffing her bag with facts to feed the hydra. One of the hydra's severed heads was tied to her belt and was both shrunken and emaciated croaking nothing in a parched whisper.

"Fancy seeing you here," I cried as I strolled across the terrazzo floor with a warm smile of welcome.

"Imagine you pilgrim in a coffee shop," she replied, her grey eyes twinkling as she patted her bag and said, "I have spent so long out with research and discovery and the hydra will be hungry."

"I do not understand why you continue to lop off the heads of the poor beasts, look at the poor beast croaking at your belt."

"You know very well that truth calls to me when I walk into the hydra cave."

As though it knew the mention of its name her sword seemed to glow and exude warmth and any of the heads making silly arguments fall to the floor. While two or more appear instantly arguing opposite sides of the same basic position.

"Nothing," croaked hydra.

'Yes," wisdom smiled looking at the head at her belt. "Except for hydra here who just never stops talking."

But pretty soon the whole hydra is distracted from the shadows in the cave.

"You are a good friend to philosophy you keep it well fed and prune it with truth," as I gave her a hug and headed out into the dusty street.

Chapter 30

We Do Not Exist

We do not exist unless there is someone who can see us existing and what we say has no meaning until someone can understand while to be surrounded by friends is constantly to have our identity confirmed. Their knowledge and care for us have the power to pull us from our numbness. True friends do not evaluate us constantly and to worldly criteria. It is the core self they are interested in and their love for us remains unaffected by our appearance or position in the social hierarchy. A handful of true friends could deliver the love and respect that even a future one may not. A friend among other things is someone kind enough to consider more of us normal than most people do.

We may share judgements with friends that would in ordinary company be censured for being too caustic, sexual, despairing, deft, clever or vulnerable. Friendship a minor conspiracy against what other people think of us as reasonable friendship being the essential component of happiness and what we normally call friendships are no more than acquaintances and familiar friendships bound by some chance or some suitability our souls support each other. On the friendship talking about souls which are mingled and confounded in so universal a blending that they efface the seam which joins them together so it cannot be found.

Chapter 31

Peace And Friendship

For some the simple life withdrawn from the tumult of politics and spent in the company of friends could be peaceful and happy and also maintain that to enjoy peace and happiness we must cultivate justice since injustice produces social conflict so if we want to be happy and find peace we should avoid political life and its stressful and dangerous entanglements. There are clear elements in the hippy dream especially in the idea that simply living apart from the mainstream is the key to peace and happiness and love but is it right to retreat while the outside world is plagued by war hate and sorrow? In philosophy terms peace love and happiness are the result of civilising processes including military and police powers.

We can enjoy this peace love and happiness because our borders are secure, our homes are comfortable, our economics are stable which sadly cannot be said for others around the world. Peace is undermined by preparation for war. Love is destroyed by oppressive hierarchies. Happiness is subverted by the demands of work, conformity and bureaucracy but it may be that military power, obedience, hierarchy and conformity are essential for peace love and happiness. It may be that the best place to find peace love and happiness is in the hippy dream with our friends. We have a goal in life and achieve peace by our ability to draw on strengths which come from our friendship with others to construct new paths.

Our friendships should become increasingly diverse and complex so that we have networks of people who support us and who are supported by us and we should also know that peace will be continually re-evaluated and redefined rather than static and stagnant. It does not preclude struggle, conflict sorrow or pain but it gives us the emotional, physical and relational resources to overcome and flourish in spite of and because of all the difficulties. Interpersonal peace requires a balance between care for ourselves and care for others. Truth and insight happen through friendships in which we are challenged and supported and another important component of interpersonal peace is humility.

Humility recognises that we can grow, act and respond so although philosophy frequently characterises the pursuit of truth and insight happens through friendships that have pushed us to see what we would otherwise ignore or resist to create peace. Peace literally agreement making happens when a sense of community shared purpose and mutual interest all prevail over divisiveness opposing purposes and disunity. This is why people of common heritage shared values and familiar experiences usually find it easier to be at peace with one another of different traditions, religious cultures or ethnicities getting along by self control with groups comes more naturally when groups are or seem to be more alike than foreign.

The challenge is to foster a sense of community of participation sufficiently strong to overcome divisiveness differences and misunderstandings. This harmonious ideal is anchored by a spirit of tolerance and respect where differences are seen as enhancing possibilities for human experience rather than as threats which must be dominated or destroyed. We try to internalise practice to foster within ourselves and without our community. All of us succeed at living peacefully to some extent in any context dependent on comparative behaviour perhaps with immediate family, close friends, co-workers, religious people, neighbours, customers and so on.

One of the fascinating features of positive peace when it happens is that it rarely occurs to those living peacefully. That they are making peace is simply how they live and interact. It is habitual, taken for granted and nearly invisible. Unfortunately there are limits to our peacefulness and few of us can take co-operation for granted on how we can interact with everyone. The mark of truly peaceful people is whether their methods of dealing with peace breakers are consistent with their visions of peace. Of course the most obvious peaceful method to resolve conflict and achievement is discussion. Peace means the presence of harmonious and co-operative social order. Every step towards peace is about us as individuals with particular choices to make and about our friendships with others and we achieve our goals by drawing on our strengths, our intelligence, our strength of will, our exuberance and our optimism but our ability to draw on these strengths comes from our friendships with others.

Peace, love and happiness and if we were all more peaceful and loving we would be happier and being happy it would be easier to live in peace with others, as they are central to the overall conception of what constitutes a good life and concrete to what it means to be human as our souls in friendship support each other. Having friends is the best part of life. Being surrounded by friends is constantly to have our identity confirmed and we do not truly exist without our friends and having the combining of our souls. Peace and friendships are vital in the hippy dream with our friends in peace, love and happiness and we need to take it seriously in order to live a good life.

Chapter 32

Moral Evolution

The next stage of human evolution is upon us. It is just a matter of time. We are the species that transforms and transcends and it is what we are. It never stops but we are also the species that is conscious of its own evolution and we must use this unique gift to direct that evolution in such a way as to transcend our moral limitations not just our biological ones. Achieving practical immortality for example is not simply a case of replacing our disposable physical form with a more durable one. It is about achieving a state of grace in which we can honestly say that we are able to live with ourselves for eternity. In order to achieve such a state of grace we must embrace the notion that our common humanity is forged from the strands of our interacting differences and we must accept that the psychedelic fabric of our transcendental unification will be woven from the multi-coloured nature of our diversity.

It is not enough for us to simply preach inclusiveness we also have to fight inequality by reorganising the re-engineering of polarising dynamics that are individual modern capitalism and consumerism. We need to do this not simply to redress the inequality of modern society but to defend ourselves from the looming bifurcation of our species. If we do not act now we may one day be forced to accept that we have engineered an irreversible evolutionary divergence on a planet whose ability to sustain life has been terminally depleted by a system which uses its resources to develop the technology to transcend its limitations and leave.

We need our humanity, our friendships and others above technological advances which could wipe us all out and trigger a social disruption. Predictions of a technological singularity and the arrival of the future looks terrifying and the pace of change is going to be astonishingly quick that we will not be able to follow it unless we enhance our own intelligence. The exponential rising curve of our technology suddenly becomes the exponential rising curve of ourselves. Our future will arise from a convergence between artificial intelligence, robots, virtual reality, biotech and mono-technology and it will be depend too on the interesting differences that make up human culture and social harmony.

Chapter 33

Party Gatherings And Events

It is a sentiment that you should keep your friends close but your enemies closer and that implies there is no such thing as genuine friendship at all. However the essence of friendship should be a rejection of politicking, the withstanding of caprices, the wandering over and remaining loyal to be a celebration of the fidelity among equals of the bond of true friendship that does not allow itself to be broken by a better offer. Neither friend in a relationship may be better than the other which is why the relationship between friends so often borrows its model from that between brother and sister who know too much about each other to act superior for very long.

Within a fellowship the pearl of perfection consists in friendship for all forms of it which are foraged or fostered by pleasure or by public or private necessity and therefore so much friendship and so much the less friendship are so much the less beautiful and noble in that they bring in some purpose of fruition other than the friendship itself. It is precisely because friendship has the potential to be one of the loftiest experiences of all. Whenever you recruit friends to some purpose, end or fruition other than the friendship itself, you are not making friends but hiring accomplices.

Get-togethers that convene people in the garden of friendship while allowing in just a scent of Eros to subtly perfume the air that seems the essence of the get together. Even the gathering that assembles long standing couples who are all friends has the ability to re-open the enquiry that let them pair off in the first place to sustain the normally dormant question about each other's attributes as a mate but not the inclination to pursue it. This is what makes a party gathering rather than an appointment, a gathering that turns a blind eye to the passing around of an ounce of sexual risk even if it's tacitly understood no one will partake. For no doubt recalculating the monetary worth of individual friends you have long known the sum will usually work out the same and yet the party is about reissuing of your stake as if you were touting for love as a gesture towards the erotic that is understood will not be further investigated so the modern day guide to going to a party might include the following advice.

There are no rules, a party cannot take off unless you accept a level of uncertainty and unless you arrive with the willingness to be tossed around on its currents that will pitch you into random conversations. Otherwise it is not a party but an assignment, but that said you do not want to end up blinded by alliances made behind your back. The very least is you ought to be aware of what is going on, if there is any damage coming your way try to see it coming and if that sounds far too cynical rather than establishing a scale of fear according to which people can find their place in the pecking order a party like friendship itself ought to be the epitome of equable relations among well intentioned peers.

Going to a party or gathering means laying aside your ambitions and throwing yourself into an event with no purpose beyond cementing that equality and you should arrive naked so to speak not because you are going to indulge your lust but because you are not dressing yourself as any better than anyone else. In its almost erotic atmosphere you might be tempted to pair off with someone new but you would do better remaining a friend to all. At a party defences will be softened but the feelings do not have to be sexual more a sizing up to the flattering social penetration of guest by guest to the inquisitive exploration of each character's contours.

In fact anything explicitly sexual at a party would make it something else, a theatre of satisfaction rather than of desire, of fruition rather that has no further fruit in it whereas the appealingly tensile quality of a good party escalates into a saturation of other indulgences, drinking, dancing, etc, and sex should remain a private sport since it pushes against the partying exclusiveness egalitarian democratic inward pull. A party can be the anteroom but never the bedroom, a touching but not a crossing of the threshold.

Philosophy of Friendship

The party is a ritual which suggests it is real and is not the connubial but nor is it a denial of it, you have all agreed to be friends while recognising that different couples might have formed out of the people in the room. According to biblical traditions love can be subdivided into friendship – philia, and spiritual or emotional – agape.

Chapter 34

Feminist Friendships

Views in feminist philosophy pick up the idea of caring benevolent concern and interest as crucial and as trumping the potentially conflicting idea of justice with a connotation of indifferent or equal concern for others. The mutual relationship of care distinctive of friendship is partial, preferential and voluntary and its value to the parties is the driver for saying that in a competition between universalist views as embodied in the idea of impartial justice and the particularism of the care perspective the latter wins.

Obviously though a distinction needs to be drawn between friendship as a theatre of caring and other relationships where a familiar difficulty arises – not all and perhaps not most caring relationships are mutual, as mutuality in caring and respect for justice are not merely compatable but actually a further constituent of what it is for a relationship to be a form of friendship. It is almost exclusively in recent discussion that female perspectives on friendship have been added to the debate and this is a function of the suppression of women's voices in most of history and looking back at the landscape of interest in this the tone is almost wholly masculine.

Friendship of men has enjoyed glory and acclaim but the friendship of women has usually been mocked, belittled and falsely interpreted and yet to generalise the attestation of anecdote and experience is that friendship between women can be and often is closer, more enduring, more confidential and more supportive, more intimate, more powerful and complete than is customary among men whose friendships are often predicated on doing things together rather than saying things to each other making taciturnity about private and intimate matters with attachments instead to external matters, to careers, sports, news, practical interests and the like.

Loyalty and affection between women is a noble relationship which far from being impoverished actually enhances and what is surprising now is their apologetic character. Even here loyalty and affection between women is not allowed to stand in its own right but requires justification in terms of those who have prior claim on that loyalty and affection and the obvious reason is that until very recently it has been nigh impossible for women to be defined otherwise than in connection with the roles that women play.

Chapter 35

Friendship Examined

We think we know what philosophers mean when they say that friendship is an intrinsic good – good in itself not for any other reason than that it is good thus excluding the good things that friendship brings us and does for us for mention of them introduces the idea of instrumentality from which high mindedness recoils. This recoil can be justified in light of examination of examples of dishonest or deceitful cases of false friendship which has a particularly bad name in that it trades on the bond of trust, constitutively implicit in friendship in order to betray it for the advantage of the betrayer but friendships can be of any kinds of mutual usefulness without being hypocritical or deceitful and friendships can and often do grow from the mutual help and advantage that interpersonal relationships supply. In fact in the practice of life it is hard to see how any friendship can be characterised as other than a trade off because it is typically a trade off of a very good and pleasing kind at the very least giving pleasure, comfort and happiness to the parties when they are enacting their friendship together.

Why is friendship good and valuable? By listing the pleasure, the fun, the utility and the advantage that comes from a strong mutual liking between people who are interested in each other's welfare and benefit and who help each other because of that interest. All these things are good too whose possession enhances the quality of our experience of life, but there is of course more. We say that friends that share things not just pleasure but knowledge and experience and also burdens and difficulties and these latter prompt the thought that comfort, solace and sympathy are profoundly valuable gifts of friendship in times of trouble which no one seeks a friend for. We do not think to make some friends just in case in future we suffer grief or illness and might need them as the chief reason for having them. It is likely that we never consider this when making friends but for which having a friend is an intrinsic good.

When talk of sharing wavers and sentiment arises it principally means experience – the magazine version would probably focus on laughter and tears, holidays, secrets, but does not often mean actual sharing and one good thing about friendship which has survived changes in social conventions is that it is a resource of guidance and connection. A loyal friend whom one trusts can tell us when we are going wrong, reprove us, advise us, and suggest a course of action when we are wavering in a dilemma, can stand up for us or do something for us when we need an ally. If you think of someone who has no friends you see what can happen, a human being like a neglected garden may become rather overgrown quite literally, unkempt, unsocial, introverted after a bit, eccentric or half mad.

Social intercourse keeps people quite literally clean and reasonably polite, sane and functional. How much more so does having a good friend help to keep people functioning in ways they often do not if left in the void of friendlessness. So such are some of the goods of friendship but friendships have their negative sides, aspects and dangers too. One is that when we make friends we contract for grief as inevitably one of any pair is going to be bereft of the other by death or divorce by the drifting apart that time brings as people and circumstances change. In the latter case the drifting apart might be mutual, scarcely noticed and no great sorrow to either but death or a quarrel or a betrayal these cause suffering and do harm.

The pangs of betrayal in friendships have their own special character and hostility friendship becomes enmity also some friendships can be ruined by becoming sexual. There is a general point which is that whereas there are not rational good things, pleasant sensations being an example, there is nothing good about irrational things than friendship is harmful. Another matter that merits consideration is the other self. The idea of merging of the two selves into one is an effort to emphasise unity of outlook and interest of agreement not of the loss of self in another self or the submerging of two identities into a corporate or joint identity for this would be to deny much of what is good and important about friendship in the first place. The quickest way to make this point is to remember that we value autonomy, self determination and the construction and enhancement of a personal identity as very high goods in themselves.

To honour these things in another is to be a friend to that other and to respect the autonomy of another the right to the final say in important decisions and choices is to be a good friend. To want to subsume that separateness to deny or nudge it too closely is to lose sight of the good of individuality and in fact the idea of two or more individuals whose differences are complementary and interesting, who respect each other as different and whose differences are accepted, tolerated, admired or honoured, is the very stuff of mutual friendship. The very idea of a bond of sharing, of giving mutuality is predicated on the idea of a duality or more. It seems essential to friendship that it should be a relationship between others as the central notion of friendship remains the close mutual personal link between two or more but a few people.

Personal friendship demands a great deal more thought because it requires a degree of knowledge and understanding of two different things of the other sufficient to make one's agency towards him or her apt and it also involves understanding what one is in for so to speak though in a reductive or calculating sense. Accepting, tolerating and sympathising with a friend involves a group of their feelings and hopes including the unrealistic ones because one has to beat time ready to deal with them just as one hopes one's friends will cope with one's own. It has been well said that no single person can meet all one's needs and interests and the problem this raises is that it frustrates any attempt to give a single neat definition of friendship.

The opportunity it offers is that friendships can be explained by examples so that by drawing from discussions of a friendship and cases of it one can illustrate its various aspects and see how they reveal through the veil of differences one of the most supreme values that make life worth living. That is why we turn from the abstractions of the philosophers to the makers of myth and story and the written and writers of history and its personal form biography to have a chance of seeing individual pebbles in the mosaic so that when we step back to see the whole even if we do not see it differently we see it true and cementing that friendship is far more a matter of emotion than rationality but nevertheless in philosophy because philosophy understands in its broadest sense at the mature conversation that humankind has with itself about the things that matter most to it – there has long been discussion about friendship as among the best and the most desirable of human relationships.

Chapter 36

In Conclusion

Friendship will always be the key component of humanity and friendship is the fascinating yet complex topic. Friendship comes in a variety of categories and types and the meaning of friendship varies a great deal as the nature of it appears more complicated than the trifold categorisations depict. Also there are many sub categories but there is a magical aspect to friendship which has provided much inspiration to many people especially those specific artisans and it is part of what makes for Eudaimonia which connects to the nature of what it means to be human alongside philia to a personal bond. Friendship must be cultivated although the number of them is necessarily finite. In order to be happy we also need good fortune and skill.

The two stories recounted showcase some categories of friendship and the circumstances and repercussions resulting from such friendships. Within educational establishments friendship has become an inspiration and its benefits esteemed. It seems there are four dimensions of friendship and these create a new way for seeing, thinking and acting and could be transforming. By taking friendship seriously especially in the educational environment means moving beyond contemporary ideas of education and through nurturing friendship, education would become more than it is. Friendship with God creates a problem to a lot of people more so as differences in status rules out any possibility of comradeship and to be in a friendship with God and the supernatural the virtue of charity is required. Confucius took joy in associating with those who shared his values.

The friendship between philosophy and science has always been a contentious one and an issue. At the end of the day there is no philosophy without science and there is no science at all without philosophy The most important of all friendships is the friendship with self and according to philosophy it is vital.

The central human question in cultivating friendships is, how should we live? However we were never intended to walk alone and a feature of a good life involves concern for others. There is also a special friendship between philosopher and photographer as they both share the spotlight. Since the word philosophy means love of wisdom it stands to reason that philosophy is the friend of wisdom and being totally philosophical is to truly love wisdom in openness to the specificities more than any other theory. At best it is a friendly acquaintance and if wisdom is no friend of philosophy, who else will vanquish life's futility?

In conclusion, we all need friends …

www.ingramcontent.com/pod-product-compliance
Lightning Source LLC
LaVergne TN
LVHW011427080426
835512LV00005B/303